COLOUR GUIDE TO SPRING WILDFLOWERS OF WESTERN AUSTRALIA

Part 3
Esperance and the Wheatbelt

Eddy Wajon

WAJON PUBLISHING COMPANY
2001

Books in the series

Colour Guide to Spring Wildflowers of Western Australia

Part 1:   Kalbarri and the Goldfields (1999)
Part 2:   Perth and the Southwest (2000)
Part 3:   Esperance and the Wheatbelt (2001)

Text and photographs copyright © Johannes Edmund Wajon 2001

All rights reserved. No part of this book may be reproduced or transmitted in any form by any means, electronic, electrical, mechanical, chemical, optical or otherwise, including photocopying and via the Internet, or by any information storage or retrieval system, without the written permission of the publisher, except for brief passages quoted by a reviewer in a newspaper, magazine or on the Internet.

ISBN 0 9577817 17

First published in 2001
Wajon Publishing Company
16 Eckersley Heights, Winthrop, Western Australia 6150
Phone +61-8-9310-2936
e-mail: wajonpub@wantree.com.au

Designed by Rebecca Machin, Donna Wajon and Lisa Brown
Typeset by key2design, Perth, Western Australia
Printed and bound by Kyodo Printing Company, Singapore

This book is dedicated to my wife, Donna. Thank you for your patience while I was taking all the photographs, your assistance in typing, and for your encouragement in finally producing the book after taking photos for so many years.

I would like to thank the Department of Conservation and Land Management of Western Australia for use of the Reference Herbarium and the FloraBase database. I would also like to thank Herbarium staff for assistance with identification, and Alex George for technical review.

Cover photograph: Raspberry Jam
Photographs on contents page (top to bottom): Barrens Regelia, Crab Claws, Orange Flame Grevillea, Pineapple Petrophile, Roe's Featherflower, Purple-veined Spider Orchid, Handsome Wedge-pea.

CONTENTS

Map of Western Australia — iv

Index to map of Western Australia — v

Map of Esperance and the Wheatbelt — vi

Index to map of Esperance and the Wheatbelt — vii

Flora roads — vii

How to use this book — viii

The Flowers — 1

Red flowers	1
Pink and mauve flowers	21
Orange and brown flowers	37
Yellow flowers	47
White flowers	75
Green and black flowers	97
Blue and purple flowers	101

List of multi-coloured wildflowers — 113

Index — 116

Selected reading — 120

Map of Western Australia

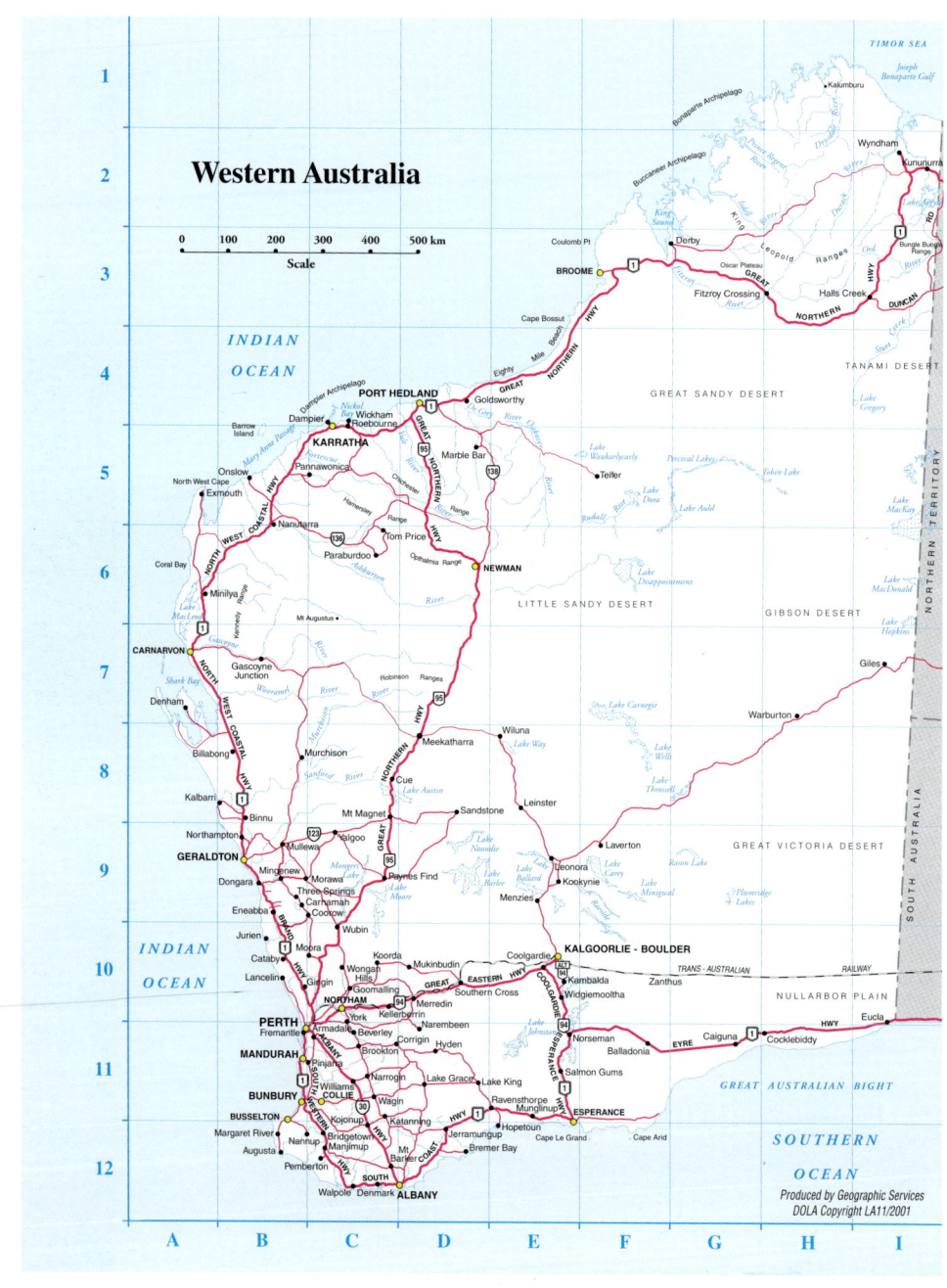

Index to map of Western Australia

TOWNS

Albany	D12	Hopetoun	E12	Murchison	B8
Armadale	C11	Hyden	D11	Nannup	C12
Augusta	B12	Jerramungup	D12	Nanutarra	B5
Balladonia	F11	Jurien	B10	Narembeen	D11
Billabong	B8	Kalbarri	B8	Narrogin	C11
Bremer Bay	D12	Kalgoorlie	E10	Newman	D6
Bridgetown	C12	Kambalda	E10	Norseman	E11
Brookton	C11	Karratha	C5	Northam	C10
Broome	F3	Katanning	C11	Northampton	B9
Bunbury	B11	Kellerberrin	C10	Onslow	B5
Busselton	B11	Kojonup	C12	Paraburdoo	C6
Caiguna	G11	Kookynie	E9	Paynes Find	C9
Cape Arid	F12	Koorda	C10	Pemberton	C12
Cape Le Grand	F12	Lake Grace	D11	Perth	B11
Carnamah	B9	Lake King	D11	Pinjarra	C11
Carnarvon	A7	Lancelin	B10	Port Hedland	D4
Cocklebiddy	H11	Laverton	F9	Ravensthorpe	E11
Collie	C11	Leinster	E8	Salmon Gums	E11
Coolgardie	E10	Leonora	E9	Sandstone	D8
Coorow	C9	Mandurah	B11	Shark Bay	A7
Corrigin	C11	Manjimup	C12	Southern Cross	D10
Cue	C8	Marble Bar	D5	Telfer	F5
Dampier	C4	Margaret River	B12	Three Springs	B9
Denham	A7	Meekatharra	D8	Wagin	C11
Denmark	C12	Menzies	E9	Walpole	C12
Dongara	B9	Merredin	D10	Warburton	H7
Eneabba	B9	Mingenew	B9	Widgiemooltha	E10
Esperance	E11	Minilya	A6	Williams	C11
Eucla	I10	Moora	C10	Wiluna	E8
Exmouth	A5	Morawa	B9	Wongan Hills	C10
Gascoyne Junction	B7	Mount Barker	C12	Wubin	C10
Geraldton	B9	Mount Magnet	C8	Wyndham	I2
Giles	I7	Mukinbudin	D10	Yalgoo	C9
Gingin	B10	Mullewa	B9	York	C10
Goomalling	C10	Munglinup	E11	Zanthus	F10

Map of Esperance and the Wheatbelt

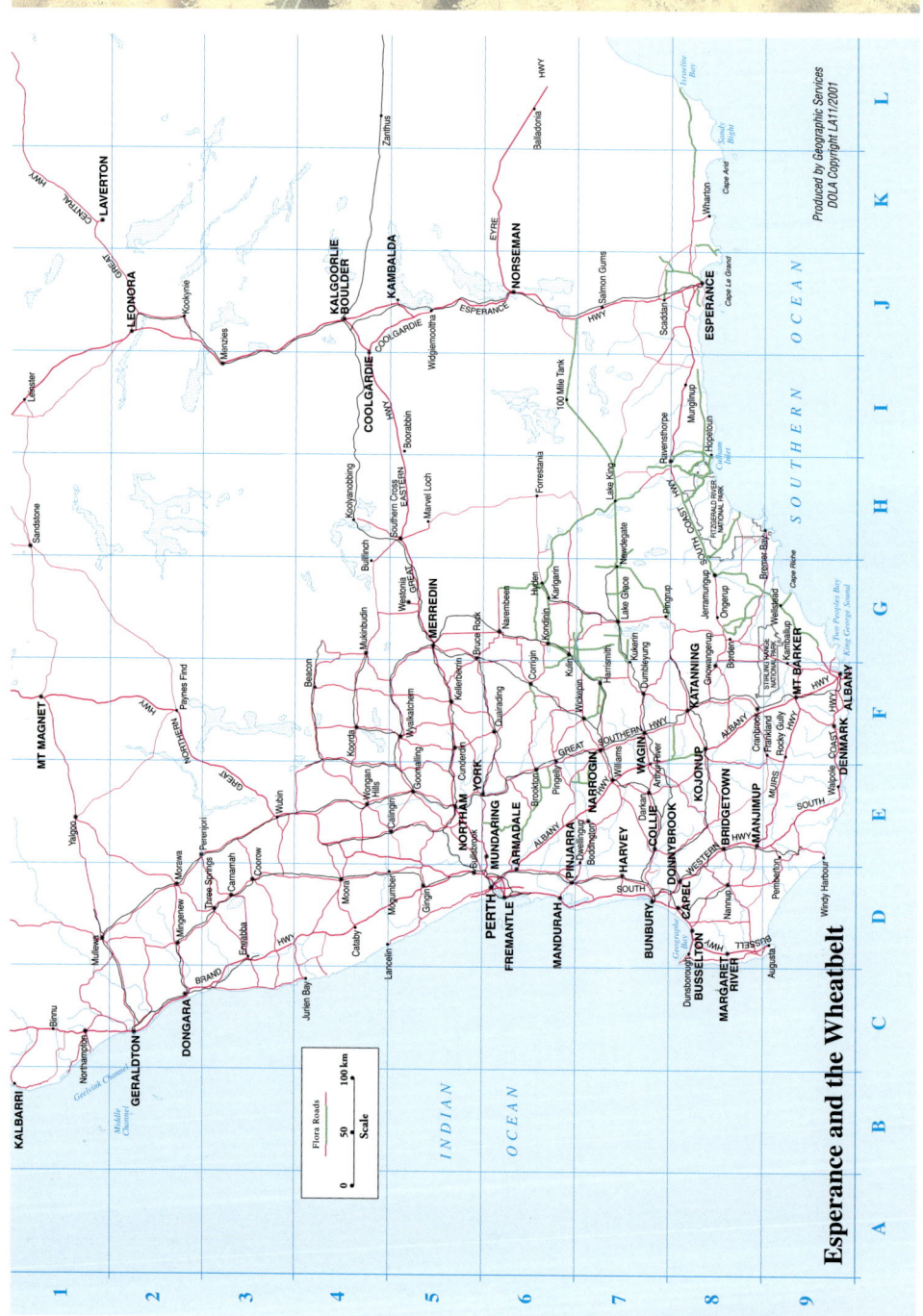

Index to map of Esperance and the Wheatbelt

TOWNS

Albany	F9	Dunsborough	D8	Lake King	H7	Perenjori	E2
Armadale	D6	Eneabba	D3	Lancelin	D4	Perth	D6
Augusta	D9	Esperance	J8	Laverton	K1	Pinjarra	D6
Balladonia	L6	Fitzgerald River	H8	Leinster	I1	Pingrup	G7
Beacon	F4	Forrestania	H6	Leonora	J2	Quairading	F6
Boddington	E7	Frankland	F9	Mandurah	D6	Ravensthorpe	H8
Boorabbin	I5	Geraldton	C2	Manjimup	E8	Rocky Gully	F9
Borden	G8	Gingin	D5	Margaret River	D8	Salmon Gums	J7
Bremer Bay	H8	Gnowangerup	F8	Menzies	I3	Sandstone	H1
Bridgetown	E8	Goomalling	E5	Merredin	G5	Scaddan	J7
Brookton	E6	Harrismith	F7	Mingenew	D2	Southern Cross	H5
Bruce Rock	G5	Harvey	D7	Mogumber	D5	Stirling Range	F9
Bullsbrook	D5	Hopetoun	I8	Moora	D4	Three Springs	D3
Bunbury	D7	Hyden	G6	Morawa	D2	Two Peoples Bay	G9
Busselton	D8	Jerramungup	G8	Mount Barker	F9	Wagin	F7
Calingiri	E5	Jurien	C4	Mount Magnet	F1	Walpole	E9
Cape Arid	K8	Kalbarri	B1	Mukinbudin	G4	Wellstead	G9
Cape Le Grand	J8	Kalgoorlie	J4	Mullewa	D1	Westonia	G5
Cape Riche	G9	Kambalda	J5	Mundaring	E6	Wharton	K8
Carnamah	D3	Kamballup	F9	Munglinup	I8	Wickepin	F7
Cataby	D4	Karlgarin	G6	Nannup	D8	Widgiemooltha	J5
Collie	E7	Katanning	F8	Narembeen	G6	Williams	E7
Coolgardie	I4	Kellerberrin	F5	Narrogin	F7	Windy Harbour	E9
Coorow	D3	Kojonup	F8	Newdegate	G7	Wongan Hills	E4
Corrigin	F6	Kondinin	G6	Norseman	J6	Wubin	E3
Cranbrook	F8	Kookynie	J2	Northam	E5	Wyalkatchem	F5
Darkan	E7	Koolyanobbing	H4	Northampton	C1	Yalgoo	E1
Denmark	F9	Koorda	F4	100 mile Tank	I6	York	E6
Dongara	C2	Kukerin	F7	Ongerup	G8	Zanthus	L4
Donnybrook	D8	Kulin	G6	Paynes Find	F2		
Dumbleyung	F7	Lake Grace	G7	Pemberton	E9		

FLORA ROADS

E6	Yarra Rd, Dale	G6-H7	Hyden-Lake King Rd	H7	Lake King-Ravensthorpe Rd
E6	Boyagin Rd, Brookton	G7	Burngup Rd South, Newdegate	H7-I7	Cascades Rd, Lake King
E6	Brookton H'way			H7-J6	Lake King-Norseman Rd
E7	Tomingley Rd, Dryandra	G7	Commonwealth Rd, Kulin	H8	Hamersley Drive, Hopetoun
E7	Wandering-Narrogin Rd, Narrogin	G7	Jarring Rd, Lake Grace	H8	John Forrest Track, Hopetoun
		G7	Kukerin-Lake Grace Rd	H8	Moir Track, Ravensthorpe
E7	York-Williams Rd, Narrogin	G7	Newdegate North Rd	H8	Mt Desmond Rd, Ravensthorpe
F6	Brookton-Corrigin Rd, Corrigin	G7	Newdegate-Pingrup Rd		
		G7	Old Lake Grace Rd, Kukerin	H8	Quiss Rd-Pabelup Track, Jerramungup
F6-G6	Corrigin-Kulin Rd	G7	Tarin Rock Rd North, Kukerin		
F7	Old Line Rd, Harrismith	G7-G6	Hopkin's Rd, Kulin	H8-I8	Hopetoun-Ravensthorpe Rd
F7	Wickepin-Harrismith Rd	G7-H7	Lake Grace-Lake King Rd	I8	Springdale Rd, Hopetoun
F7-G6	Dudinin-Kulin Rd	G7-H7	Magenta Rd, Newdegate	J7	Speddingup Rd East
F8	Albany H'way, Kojonup	G8	Nightwell Rd, Borden	J7	Wittenoom Hills Rd, Esperance
F8	Robinson Rd, Woodanilling	G8	Ongerup-Boxwood Hill Rd		
G6	Bendering Reserve/Worland Rd, Hyden	G8	Toompup South Rd, Ongerup	J8	Dempster Rd, Esperance
				J8	Telegraph Rd, Esperance
G6	Hyden Rd, Hyden	G9	Sandalwood Rd, Cape Riche	K8	Cape Le Grand Rd
G6	Kondinin-Hyden Rd	G9-H8	South Coast H'way	K8	Lucky Bay Rd
G6	Kulin-Kondinin Rd	H7	Floater Rd, Ravensthorpe	K8-L8	Fisheries Rd, Wharton

How to use this book

Western Australia has more than 12,000 species of flowering plants, making it one of the most botanically diverse areas in the world. Many of these grow in the south west of Western Australia. This guide contains photographs of 224 of the most common (and some not so common) wildflowers which can be found from July to November in the area between Perth, Albany, Cape Arid and Hyden. Many of these wildflowers are also found in areas as far apart as Kalbarri, Kalgoorlie and Augusta. You will also see other wildflowers that are not shown in this book. Some of these may be shown in Parts 1 and 2 of this series, which cover Kalbarri and the Goldfields, and Perth and the Southwest respectively.

The wildflowers in this book are grouped by colour. The sequence of colours is that of the colours of the rainbow, i.e. red, orange, yellow, green and blue. Pink flowers follow the red flowers and white flowers follow the yellow flowers. Mauve flowers are included with pink, brown flowers are included with orange, cream flowers are included with white, black flowers are included with green, and purple or lilac flowers are included with blue. There is a strip of colour on the edge of each page which identifies the colour section. Some flowers are multi-coloured; other flowers may come in a variety of colours. Only one colour form is shown, but other colour forms are cross-referenced in the index. Multi-coloured flowers are placed in the section of the most obvious colour.

Within each colour section, the flowers are arranged approximately alphabetically by scientific name. A common name is given for each plant. Most of these common names are derived from the book "Common and Aboriginal Names of Western Australian Plant Species" by E.M. Bennett. The time of flowering, and how common the plant is, are indicated. How common the plant is refers to how abundant it is in the places where it grows. Very common means that many plants are present in an area and it should be very easy to find.

The distribution of the plant is indicated by the main towns which bound the area where it may be found. The distribution indicates where the plant may be found, but it may not be present everywhere within that area. Where a plant grows is controlled by many factors including habitat and soil type. This is indicated in the text. The place where the photograph featured in the book was taken is the first entry in the box where you can record your own observations. All towns are shown in the maps at the front of the book. The maps also show main roads along which you can see a good wildflower display.

When you find a wildflower, turn to the relevant colour section and scan the photographs for a flower that looks similar. Compare the real wildflower with the photograph. Read the description which describes the flower and plant in very simple terms. Note the size and shape of the leaves, and where the plant grows. If it does not seem to fit the description, look in the list of multi-coloured flowers because your plant may be shown in another colour section. Look at the list under the colour of the plant you are trying to identify, and turn to the photos of the flowers on the pages indicated. If you vaguely know the name of the plant, you might try going to the index of common or scientific names. If you are still not able to identify it, look in the books in Part 1 or 2 of this series. As a last resort, consult one of the books listed in the references.

DATE	PLACE
9/00	Cape Le Grand
10/05	Esperance

SEPTEMBER-FEBRUARY
UNCOMMON

RED KANGAROO PAW

Anigozanthos rufus

Woodland and heath in sand. Cranbrook to Wellstead, Cape Arid and Lake King. Herb 0.2–1.5 m high. Several groups of six to eight woolly red to purple flowers 3–5 cm long on woolly red stems 1.5 m long. Flat, sword-shaped leaves 50–80 cm long x 1–2 cm wide, mostly at base of plant.

DATE	PLACE
12/91	Fitzgerald River National Park

SEPTEMBER-DECEMBER
COMMON

RED ANTHOTIUM

Anthotium rubriflorum

Heath in sand or gravel. Calingiri to Jerramungup, Ravensthorpe and Lake King. Herb 5–20 cm high. Red flowers 10–15 mm across in a head 5–10 cm across. Toothed, spear-shaped leaves 3–5 cm long x 5 mm wide, all at base of plant.

DATE	PLACE
9/00	*Kondinin*

FEBRUARY-DECEMBER   UNCOMMON

Woodland and heath in sand or gravel. Wyalkatchem to Brookton, Lake Grace, Lake King and Boorabbin.
Shrub 0.25–1.5 m high. Hairy bright red to pink flowers 20–25 mm long with smooth tips. Leaves 10 mm long divided into three soft, flat, hairy leaflets 5–10 mm long x 2 mm wide, crowded at end of branches.

LITTLE WOOLLYBUSH
Adenanthos argyreus

DATE	PLACE
10/96	*Karlgarin*

JANUARY-NOVEMBER   COMMON

Woodland and heath in sand or gravel. Narrogin to Cranbrook, Hopetoun, Ravensthorpe and Hyden.
Shrub 0.25–1.5 m high. Hairy bright red to pink flowers 25–30 mm long with hairy tips. Leaves 10–15 mm long divided into three to seven soft, hairy, needle-like leaflets 5–10 mm long x 2 mm wide.

WHEATBELT WOOLLYBUSH
Adenanthos flavidiflorus

DATE	PLACE
10/00	Lucky Bay

AUGUST–APRIL
VERY COMMON

GRANITE WOOLLYBUSH
Adenanthos sericeus subsp. *sphalma*

Heath in sand on rocky outcrops. Cape Le Grand to Cape Arid.
Shrub 0.5–2 m high. Hairy bright red to orange flowers 10–30 mm long. Leaves 3 cm long divided into six to fifteen soft, hairy, needle-like leaflets 5–30 mm long x 0.5–1 mm wide.

DATE	PLACE
10/95	East Mount Barren

AUGUST–MAY   COMMON

Heath on rock. Fitzgerald River National Park.
Shrub 0.5–2 m high. Red to pink and cream flowers 20–40 mm long x 5–10 mm wide. Pointed, cupped, oval leaves 10–25 mm long x 10–15 mm wide.

VEINED-LEAF JUG FLOWER
Adenanthos venosus

TAMMA
Allocasuarina campestris

DATE	PLACE
9/00	Ravensthorpe
09/07	Gt. N. Highway, S of New Norcia

JULY–SEPTEMBER VERY COMMON

Woodland in sand or gravel. Billabong to Gingin, Cape Riche, Cape Arid and Kalgoorlie.
Shrub 1–3 m high. Hairy, globular, red female flowers 3–7 mm across; brown male flowers in spike 5–30 mm long x 2–3 mm wide at end of branches on same or separate plant. Branches of 5–15 mm long segments tipped with eight leaves 0.5–1 mm long. Holey, brown, cylindrical nut 20–40 mm long x 10–15 mm wide.

BLOATED SHEOAK
Allocasuarina microstachya

DATE	PLACE
9/00	Corrigin

AUGUST–OCTOBER UNCOMMON

Heath in sand or gravel. Dongara to Perth, Cranbrook, Munglinup and Boorabbin.
Shrub 0.1–1 m high. Wavy, globular, red female flowers 2–5 mm across; spiky, brown male flowers 0.5–3 mm long x 1–2 mm wide on separate plant. Four-sided swollen branches of 2–6 mm long segments tipped with four leaves 0.5–1.5 mm long. Smooth, grey, egg-shaped nut 10–15 mm long x 5–10 mm wide.

DATE	PLACE
9/00	*Lucky Bay*

SEPTEMBER   VERY COMMON

Woodland on rocky slopes. Walpole to Cape Arid and Cranbrook.
Shrub 0.5–5 m high. Hairy, globular, red or orange female flowers 10–15 mm across; hairy, brown male flowers in spike 3–8 cm long x 2–3 mm wide at end of branches on separate plant. Branches of 10–15 mm long segments tipped with ten thin hairy leaves 2–3.5 mm long. Spiky, brown nut 15–50 mm long x 15–20 mm wide.

HAIRY SHEOAK
Allocasuarina trichodon

DATE	PLACE
6/94	*Dryandra*

JANUARY-DECEMBER
UNCOMMON

SPOON-LEAVED CRANBERRY
Astroloma compactum

Woodland in sand or gravel. Calingiri to Bridgetown, Rocky Gully, Bremer Bay, Cape Arid and Kulin.
Straggly, circular, cushion shrub 2–15 cm high. Red to pink flowers 10–15 mm long x 3 mm wide with woolly tips. Crowded, toothed or hairy, spoon- or spear-shaped leaves 5–10 mm long x 2–4 mm wide, ending in a sharp point.

DATE	PLACE
9/00	East Mount Barren
10/05	East Mount Barren

SEPTEMBER-NOVEMBER AND
FEBRUARY-APRIL   COMMON

Heath in sand on rocky outcrops. Hopetoun.
Shrub 0.5–3 m high. Red flowers 3–4 cm long with smooth red to purple base in a small group on one side of branch. Crowded, needle-like leaves 20–30 mm long x 2 mm wide, ending in a sharp point. Brown nut 15 mm across.

LARGE-FRUITED CLAWFLOWER

Calothamnus macrocarpus

DATE	PLACE
10/95	East Mount Barren
10/05	Point Ann

JULY-NOVEMBER
VERY COMMON

DENSE CLAWFLOWER

Calothamnus pinifolius

Woodland and heath in sand or gravel on rocky outcrops. Cape Riche to Hopetoun and Ravensthorpe.
Shrub 0.5–3 m high. Red flowers 3–4 cm long with hairy green to grey base in spike 4–10 cm long around stem. Very prickly, crowded, needle-like leaves 15–25 mm long x 1 mm wide, ending in a sharp point. Brown nut 10 mm across.

DATE	PLACE
9/98	West Mount Barren
10/05	East Mt Barren

JULY-NOVEMBER
COMMON

BARRENS CLAWFLOWER
Calothamnus validus

Heath in sand on rocky slopes. Peaks of the Fitzgerald River National Park.
Shrub 0.5–2 m high. Red flowers 3–4 cm long with smooth red base in a small group around branch. Crowded, erect, pointed, needle-like leaves 15–30 mm long x 1 mm wide. Brown nut 10–15 mm across.

DATE	PLACE
9/00	Lucky Bay
10/05	Lucky Bay

MARCH-JULY AND
SEPTEMBER-DECEMBER
COMMON

WOOLLY CLAWFLOWER
Calothamnus villosus

Heath in sand on rocky hills. Cranbrook to Cape Riche, Cape Arid and Ravensthorpe.
Shrub 0.5–1.5 m high. Red flowers 2–3 cm long with silvery hairy red base in a small group around branch. Crowded, erect, needle-like leaves 10–40 mm long x 1 mm wide, ending in a sharp point. Brown nut 10 mm across.

DATE	PLACE
9/98	Esperance

ESPERANCE KING SPIDER ORCHID
Caladenia decora

AUGUST-OCTOBER
COMMON

Heath and rock outcrops in wet areas. Bremer Bay to Cape Arid and Scaddan.
Slender plant 25–50 cm high. One to three salmon-red to brown flowers 5–15 cm long x 5–10 cm wide with long fringes on lip and thickened yellow tips to three petals. Hairy, grass-like leaf 10–20 cm long x 5–10 mm wide at base of plant.

DATE	PLACE
9/97	Woodanilling
10/05	Ravensthorpe

FRINGED MANTIS ORCHID
Caladenia falcata

SEPTEMBER-OCTOBER
COMMON

Woodland, heath and sheoak forests. Wongan Hills to York, Mount Barker, Jerramungup and Hyden.
Slender plant 20–40 cm high. One or two red, yellow and green flowers 10 cm long x 5–10 cm wide with long fringes, red tip on lip and thickened yellow tips to three petals. Hairy, grass-like leaf 10–20 cm long x 5–15 mm wide at base of plant.

DATE	PLACE
9/98	Jerramungup

SEPTEMBER-OCTOBER
UNCOMMON

LAZY SPIDER ORCHID
Caladenia multiclavia

Sheoak forests near creeks. Wongan Hills to Cranbrook, Bremer Bay, Ravensthorpe and Hyden. Slender plant 10–25 cm high. One to two red to pink flowers 5 cm long x 3 cm wide with red lumps on striped lip. Hairy, grass-like leaf 5–10 cm long x 5–10 mm wide at base of plant.

DATE	PLACE
9/98	Ongerup

SEPTEMBER-OCTOBER
UNCOMMON

SLENDER SPIDER ORCHID
Caladenia pulchra

Sheoak forests near creeks. Wubin to Bridgetown, Jerramungup and Southern Cross. Slender plant 20–40 cm high. One to three long, wispy, red flowers with yellow bases 10–15 cm long x 5–10 cm wide with short fringes on lip. Hairy, grass-like leaf 5–15 cm long x 5 mm wide at base of plant.

DATE	PLACE
9/97	Ravensthorpe

RAVENSTHORPE BOTTLEBRUSH
Beaufortia orbifolia

JANUARY-DECEMBER
COMMON

Heath in gravel. Corrigin to Ravensthorpe, Southern Cross and Merredin. Shrub 0.5–3.5 m high. Red globular flowers 5 cm across at or just below end of side branches. Crowded, round to oval leaves 5 mm across.

DATE	PLACE
10/99	Borden

AUGUST-DECEMBER   COMMON

Heath in sand or gravel. Northampton to Dunsborough, Denmark, Cape Arid and Merredin.
Erect or spreading shrub 0.15–1 m high. Red to pink, orange or yellow pea flowers 10–15 mm across in groups near ends of branches. Straight leaves 5–25 mm long x 1–4 mm wide, ending in a sharp point.

NEEDLE-LEAVED FLAME PEA
Chorizema aciculare

DATE	PLACE
10/97	Harrismith

JULY–NOVEMBER
UNCOMMON

WARTY BUSH
Chloanthes coccinea

Heath in sand or gravel. Corrigin to Frankland, Cranbrook and Lake Grace. Straggly or spreading shrub 20–80 cm high. Numerous furry, tubular red to pink flowers 20–35 mm long x 5–10 mm wide, woolly at base. Warty, woolly, oblong leaves 5–15 mm long x 1–3 mm wide, continuing down stem.

DATE	PLACE
10/95	East Mount Barren
10/05	Hyden rad

SEPTEMBER–JANUARY
COMMON

SPLENDID FOXGLOVE
Pityrodia exserta

Heath in sand or clay on rocky slopes. Hyden to Jerramungup, Bremer Bay, Cape Arid and Forrestania.
Sprawling shrub 10–50 cm high. Furry, tubular red to pink flowers 25–35 mm long x 15–20 mm wide. Warty, woolly, oblong leaves 10–25 mm long x 1 mm wide.

DATE	PLACE
10/96	Karlgarin

STAR-LEAF GREVILLEA
Grevillea asteriscosa

MAY AND
AUGUST-NOVEMBER
UNCOMMON

Heath in gravel or near rocky outcrops. Bruce Rock to Corrigin, Lake Grace and Narembeen.
Shrub 0.5–2.5 m high. Four to six hairy red flowers 10 mm long in head 2–5 cm across. Prickly, hairy, star-shaped leaves 5–10 mm long x 10–20 mm wide.

DATE	PLACE
10/96	Lake King

HUEGEL'S GREVILLEA
Grevillea huegelii

JUNE AND
SEPTEMBER-FEBRUARY
UNCOMMON

Woodland and heath in sand or gravel. Wubin to Moora, Cranbrook, Wellstead, Cape Arid and Zanthus.
Shrub 0.5–3 m high. Many red, pink, orange or yellow flowers 20-30 mm long in circular head 2.5–5 cm across. Prickly leaves 1–6 cm long x 1–6 cm wide, divided into many flat leaflets 5–40 mm long x 1–2 mm wide, each ending in a sharp point.

DATE	PLACE
8/96	Hyden
10/05	Ongerup road

JANUARY-DECEMBER
VERY COMMON

RED TOOTHBRUSHES
Grevillea cagiana

Woodland and heath in sand. Brookton to Kamballup, Cape Arid and Coolgardie. Shrub 1–4 m high. Many straight bright red or orange flowers 15–25 mm long with yellow or red tips and silky pink, green, yellow or orange bases in spike 2–6 cm long on one side of branch. Straight, pointed, simple or divided leaves 5–15 cm long x 1–2 mm wide.

DATE	PLACE
9/00	Scaddan
10/05	Hamersley drive

MAY-NOVEMBER
VERY COMMON

RED PAINTBRUSHES
Grevillea tetragonoloba

Woodland and heath in sand. Mount Barker to Cape Riche, Munglinup, Scaddan and Newdegate. Shrub 0.5–2.5 m high. Many bright red flowers 15–30 mm long with red tips and silky creamy-brown to brown bases leaning backwards in spike 4–12 cm long on one side of branch and not exceeding leaves. Leaves 5–15 cm long, divided into many straight, flat, pointed leaflets 3–8 cm long x 1–2 mm wide.

DATE	PLACE
9/92	Tarin Rock, Lake Grace

WAX GREVILLEA

Grevillea insignis

JULY-NOVEMBER AND JANUARY
COMMON

Woodland and heath in sand. York to Narrogin, Pingrup, Forrestania and Hyden. Shrub 1–5 m high. Many red to pink or cream flowers 10-20 mm long in head 2.5–5 cm across. Prickly, wavy, saw-toothed oval leaves 3–9 cm long x 3–4 cm wide.

DATE	PLACE
9/97	Newdegate

WOOLLY RED GREVILLEA

Grevillea pilosa

MAY-DECEMBER
COMMON

Heath in sand, gravel or clay. Hyden to Newdegate, Ravensthorpe and Forrestania. Shrub 0.5–2 m high. Many woolly red to pink flowers 20-30 mm long in head 3–5 cm long x 3–4 cm wide. Prickly, furry, wavy, saw-toothed oval or wedge-shaped leaves 1–6 cm long x 1–6 cm wide.

DATE	PLACE
9/97	East Mount Barren
10/05	Point Ann

MAY-JANUARY
VERY COMMON

TRAILING GREVILLEA
Grevillea nudiflora

Woodland and heath in sand. Kamballup to Cape Riche, Cape Arid, Salmon Gums and Jerramungup.
Prostrate, spreading or erect shrub 0.2–2 m high. Two to six red flowers 20–25 mm long, usually on trailing leafless stems up to 2.5 m long. Straight leaves 5–25 cm long x 1–5 mm wide.

DATE	PLACE
9/00	Ravensthorpe

APRIL-DECEMBER   COMMON

Woodland and heath in sand or gravel. Pingrup to Gnowangerup, Hopetoun and Lake King.
Shrub 0.5–3 m high. Many red or pink and yellow flowers 2–4 cm across on hanging zig-zag stalk 2–10 cm long. Prickly leaves 2–5 cm long x 2–6 cm wide, divided into many flat, straight or triangular leaflets 5–20 mm long x 1–15 mm wide, each ending in a sharp point.

ZIG-ZAG FLOWERED GREVILLEA
Grevillea patentiloba

DATE	PLACE
10/95	John Forrest Track

COMB-LEAVED GREVILLEA

Grevillea pectinata

JUNE-FEBRUARY
UNCOMMON

Woodland and heath in sand or gravel. Kulin to Albany, Cape Arid and Salmon Gums. Shrub 0.5–2.5 m high. Many hanging red to pink flowers 3–4 cm long in a head 4–5 cm across. Comb-like, wedge-shaped leaves 1–6 cm long x 5–35 mm wide, divided into many flat leaflets 5–25 mm long x 1–2 mm wide, each ending in a sharp point.

DATE	PLACE
9/97	Mylies Beach
10/05	Hamersley Drive

THREE-LOBED GREVILLEA

Grevillea tripartita

JANUARY-DECEMBER
COMMON

Heath in sand, clay or gravel. Pingrup to Gnowangerup, Hopetoun and Lake King. Shrub 0.5–3 m high. Many red to orange and yellow flowers 45–50 mm long in groups 5–8 cm across. Prickly leaves 1–5 cm long x 1–5 cm wide, divided into three flat, straight or triangular leaflets 1–4 cm long x 1–5 mm wide, each ending in a sharp point.

DATE	PLACE
9/00	Cape Le Grand

SEPTEMBER-NOVEMBER   COMMON

Woodland and heath on granite outcrops. Cape Le Grand to Cape Arid. Shrub 1–4 m high. Many red flowers in a cylinder 4–8 cm long x 6 cm wide at end of branches. Oblong leaves 10–20 mm long x 2–3 mm wide.

BAXTER'S KUNZEA
Kunzea baxteri

DATE	PLACE
10/95	Hyden

JUNE AND
OCTOBER-DECEMBER
UNCOMMON

GRANITE KUNZEA
Kunzea pulchella

Woodland on granite outcrops. Wubin to Wagin, Norseman, Menzies and Mount Magnet.
Shrub 0.5–3 m high. Many red flowers 25–45 mm across at end of branches. Silky oval-shaped leaves 5–15 mm long x 2–7 mm wide.

DATE	PLACE
9/00	Cape Le Grand
10/05	Point Ann

FOUR-WINGED MALLEE
Eucalyptus tetraptera

JUNE-DECEMBER
COMMON

Heath in sand. Kamballup to Cape Riche, Cape Arid and Salmon Gums. Straggly tree 1–3 m high. Red to pink flowers 3–9 cm long x 3–4 cm wide with 4-winged bud. Thick oval leaves 10–20 cm long x 4–8 cm wide.

DATE	PLACE
9/98	Fitzgerald River National Park
10/05	Cape Le Grand

RED LESCHENAULTIA
Lechenaultia formosa

JANUARY AND
APRIL-NOVEMBER
COMMON

Woodland and heath in sand, clay or gravel. Carnamah to Bridgetown, Albany, Cocklebiddy and Hyden.
Prostrate to erect, domed, cushion shrub 2–50 cm high. Red, orange or yellow flowers 10–15 mm across. Blunt, needle-like leaves 2–5 mm long x 0.5 mm wide.

DATE	PLACE
9/97	*Fitzgerald River National Park*

**JUNE AND SEPTEMBER-DECEMBER
VERY COMMON**

GRANITE BOTTLEBRUSH
Melaleuca elliptica

Woodland in sand on granite rocks. Narembeen to Corrigin, Albany, Caiguna and Zanthus.
Shrub 1–4 m high. Red flowers 20 mm long in a cylinder 45–55 mm long x 45–55 mm wide. Oval leaves 5–15 mm long x 5 mm wide.

DATE	PLACE
9/00	*Moir Track*
10/05	*Hamersley Drive*

JULY-OCTOBER   COMMON

Heath on rocky soils. Jerramungup to Bremer Bay, Hopetoun and Ravensthorpe.
Shrub 0.2–1 m high. Bell-shaped red to greeny yellow flowers 3–6 cm long x 2–5 cm wide. Flat, oval leaves 10–30 mm long x 5–8 mm wide.

QUALUP BELL
Pimelea physodes

DATE	PLACE
9/95	East Mount Barren
10/05	East Mount Barren

SEPTEMBER-NOVEMBER
VERY COMMON

Heath on rocky soil. Fitzgerald River National Park.
Shrub or tree 1–6 m high. Globular red flowers 3–5 cm across at end of branches. Soft, silky, oval, keeled leaves 10–15 mm long x 2–5 mm wide.

BARRENS REGELIA
Regelia velutina

DATE	PLACE
9/94	Dryandra

BITTER QUANDONG
Santalum murrayanum

OCTOBER-JANUARY
UNCOMMON

Woodland in sand or gravel. Wyalkatchem to Brookton, Cranbrook, Cape Arid, Zanthus and Laverton.
Shrub or tree 1–5 m high. White, yellow or green flowers 2 mm across. Hanging, bitter, orange-red fruit 15–25 mm across. Pale yellow-green, sword-shaped leaves 15–50 mm long x 2–5 mm wide, opposite or in threes and hooked at end.

DATE	PLACE
9/97	East Mount Barren
10/05	Jraalup

JANUARY-DECEMBER   COMMON

Heath in sand. Walpole to Cocklebiddy and Lake King.
Shrub 0.5–3 m high. Pink to mauve-red flowers 30–40 mm long x 5 mm wide with hairy tips. Soft, velvety or hairy, fan- or wedge-shaped leaves 10–30 mm long x 10–15 mm wide, red when new.

COASTAL JUG FLOWER

Adenanthos cuneatus

DATE	PLACE
9/90	Twertup, Fitzgerald River
	National Park

NOVEMBER-DECEMBER   UNCOMMON

Heath in sand, clay or gravel. Kamballup to Wellstead, Hopetoun, Ravensthorpe and Jerramungup.
Shrub 0.5–2 m high. Hanging pink to red or cream flowers in a cylinder 10–15 cm long x 7–10 cm wide. Wavy, prickly, saw-toothed leaves 5–15 cm long x 1–3 cm wide.

CAYLEY'S BANKSIA

Banksia caleyi

DATE	PLACE
10/97	Tarin Rock, Lake Grace

LITTLE BOTTLEBRUSH
Beaufortia micrantha

AUGUST-FEBRUARY
VERY COMMON

Heath in sand or gravel. Wongan Hills to Narrogin, Cape Riche, Cape Arid and Coolgardie.
Shrub 0.2–1 m high. Globular, pink to purple flowers 10 mm across at end of branches. Wedge-shaped leaves 0.5–1 mm long x 0.5 mm wide, laying flat on branches.

DATE	PLACE
9/00	John Forrest Track
10/05	Duke of Orleans Bay

PINK BOTTLEBRUSH
Beaufortia schaueri

MAY-JANUARY
COMMON

Heath in sand or rock. Lake Grace to Cranbrook, Cape Riche, Cape Arid and Hyden.
Shrub 0.3–1.5 m high. Globular pink flowers 15–25 mm across along branches. Crowded, oblong, flat leaves 3–7 mm long x 0.5 mm wide, mostly in bunches along side branches.

DATE	PLACE
9/98	West Mount Barren

JANUARY-DECEMBER   UNCOMMON

Heath on rock. Cranbrook to Albany, Cape Arid and Ravensthorpe.
Shrub 10–70 cm high. Pink or white flowers 10 mm across on very hairy branches. Hairy leaves 2–4 cm long with five to seven pairs of oblong or spoon-shaped leaflets 2–4 mm long x 1–2 mm wide along leaf.

MOUNTAIN BORONIA
Boronia albiflora

DATE	PLACE
10/96	Esperance

SEPTEMBER-DECEMBER
COMMON

PINK STARFLOWER
Calytrix decandra

Heath in sand. Jerramungup to Hopetoun, Cape Arid and Salmon Gums.
Shrub 10–70 cm high. Pink to purple star flowers 15–25 mm across with white or purple centres and long tails. Oblong, three-sided leaves 5–10 mm long x 1 mm wide.

DATE	PLACE
9/98	*Fitzgerald River National Park*
10/05	*Quaalup*

FEBRUARY–DECEMBER
VERY COMMON

FRINGED WAXFLOWER
Chamelaucium ciliatum

Heath. Mogumber to Albany, Cape Arid and Menzies.
Shrub 0.2-1.5 m high. Pink to white flowers turning red 5 mm across with fringed lobes under the petals. Oblong leaves 2-5 mm long x 0.5–1 mm wide.

DATE	PLACE
10/98	*Ravensthorpe*

AUGUST-NOVEMBER
COMMON

COMMON COOPERNOOKIA
Coopernookia polygalacea

Woodland and heath in sand, clay or gravel. Kukerin to Mount Barker, Cape Riche, Cape Arid, Salmon Gums and Hyden.
Shrub 20–70 cm high. Pink, blue or purple flowers 10–15 mm across. Furry, oblong leaves 10–20 mm long x 5–25 mm wide, folded over lengthwise.

DATE	PLACE
10/97	Lake Grace

SEPTEMBER-OCTOBER UNCOMMON

Heath in sand. Calingiri to Boddington, Mount Barker, Salmon Gums and Southern Cross.
Herb 5–10 cm high. Pink or white flowers 5 mm across at end of stalk 5–10 cm long. Sticky, hairy, round leaves 1–2 mm across on stalk 3–4 mm long, all at base of plant.

PEARLY SUNDEW
Drosera pycnoblasta

DATE	PLACE
9/97	East Mount Barren
10/05	Dwalip

AUGUST-NOVEMBER
COMMON

PAINTED LADY
Gompholobium scabrum

Forest and heath in sand. Gingin to Augusta, Albany, Cape Arid and Narrogin.
Shrub 0.5–2.5 m high. Pink pea flowers 15 mm across in clusters along ends of branches. Group of three blunt, needle-like leaves 5–10 mm long x 0.5–1 mm wide along branches.

DATE	PLACE
9/00	*Frenchman Peak*

MAY AND JULY–OCTOBER   COMMON

Woodland in sand or clay on granite outcrops. Scaddan to Esperance and Cape Arid.
Shrub 0.5–2 m high. Sweet smelling, pink or white flowers in clusters 2–3 cm across. Thick, needle-like leaves 2–7 cm long x 5–7 mm wide, ending in a sharp point. Oval, woody nut 15 mm long x 7 mm wide, sometimes with two horns at end.

COASTAL HAKEA

Hakea clavata

DATE	PLACE
8/96	*Hyden*

MAY–SEPTEMBER   UNCOMMON

Woodland and heath in sand. Morawa to Narrogin, Lake Grace, Salmon Gums, Norseman and Southern Cross.
Shrub to tree 2–5 m high. Pink flowers in spike 2–7 cm long x 2–4 cm wide on old part of branch. Thick, broad leaves 7–20 cm long x 5–25 mm wide with ten to twenty veins. Oval, woody nut 15–25 mm long x 1–2 cm wide with small beak at end and groove down centre.

GRASS LEAF HAKEA

Hakea multilineata

DATE	PLACE
10/97	Lake Grace
10/05	Corrigin

OCTOBER-NOVEMBER
COMMON

GARDNER'S CONEFLOWER

Isopogon gardneri

Heath in gravelly sand or clay. Corrigin to Pingrup, Hopetoun and Forrestania. Shrub 0.5–2 m high. Pink or yellow flowers 20–25 mm long in globular heads 3–4 cm across. Leaves 3–5 cm long divided into many sharp, pointed, needle-like sections 5–20 mm long x 1 mm wide.

DATE	PLACE
9/92	Tarin Rock, Lake Grace
10/05	Point Ann

AUGUST-NOVEMBER   COMMON

Heath in sand or clay. Eneabba to Collie, Denmark, Esperance, Southern Cross and York.
Shrub 0.3–2 m high. Woolly pink, yellow or white flowers in globular heads 2–4 cm across, hanging and turned to one side. Leaves 2–12 cm long often divided into many sharp, pointed needle-like sections 5–50 mm long x 1 mm wide.

NODDING CONEFLOWER

Isopogon teretifolius

DATE	PLACE
10/99	Ongerup

BRILLIANT KUNZEA

Kunzea affinis

AUGUST-OCTOBER
COMMON

Heath in sand or gravel. Borden to Cape Riche, Cape Arid and Widgiemooltha. Shrub 0.5–2.5 m high. Masses of pink to purple globular flowers 3–7 mm across at end of branches. Soft, needle-like leaves 2–10 mm long x 0.5–1 mm wide.

DATE	PLACE
10/99	Ongerup
10/05	Ongerup road

AUGUST-OCTOBER   VERY COMMON

Heath in sand. Pingrup to Bremer Bay, Hopetoun, Ravensthorpe and Forrestania.
Shrub 0.5–2 m high. Pink to purple globular flowers 5–7 mm across at end of branches. Oval or round leaves 1–3 mm long x 1 mm wide.

SLENDER KUNZEA

Kunzea jucunda

DATE	PLACE
10/97	Lake Grace

AUGUST–NOVEMBER
VERY COMMON

HAIRY TEATREE
Leptospermum roei

Heath in sand often with gravel. Wubin to Pingrup, Esperance, Zanthus and Menzies. Straggly shrub 1–3.5 m high. Pink or white flowers (very hairy white in bud) 5–10 mm across on long spreading branches. Oval to oblong leaves 5–10 mm long x 1–2 mm wide.

DATE	PLACE
9/00	Lucky Bay
10/05	Cape Le Grand

JULY–OCTOBER   VERY COMMON

Heath in sand on granite outcrops. Esperance to Cape Le Grand.
Shrub 0.5–3 m high. Silky pink to white flowers 2–3 cm across. Silvery, silky, oval leaves 10–15 mm long x 5–10 mm wide.

SILVER TEATREE
Leptospermum sericeum

DATE	PLACE
10/96	Munglinup
10/05	Hamersley Drive

AUGUST-FEBRUARY   VERY COMMON

Woodland or heath in sand or clay. Denham to Busselton, Mount Barker, Bremer Bay, Cape Arid and Southern Cross.
Shrub 0.2–2 m high. Globular pink to purple flowers 10–15 mm across. Rough, glandular, oblong leaves 5–10 mm long x 1 mm wide. Cylindrical nut 5–10 mm long x 8–10 mm wide.

ROUGH HONEYMYRTLE
Melaleuca scabra

DATE	PLACE
9/00	Cape Le Grand

AUGUST-NOVEMBER   COMMON

Woodland or heath in sand or clay. Cranbrook to Albany, Cocklebiddy and Ravensthorpe.
Shrub 0.3–2 m high. Pink to mauve flowers 2–3 mm long in spike 2–20 cm long growing out of thickened branches. Blunt, needle-like leaves 3–4 mm long x 1 mm wide. Round nut 2–3 mm across embedded in branch.

CORKY HONEYMYRTLE
Melaleuca suberosa

DATE	PLACE
9/00	Cape Le Grand
10/05	Juaalup

AUGUST-FEBRUARY   VERY COMMON

Coastal sand dunes and limestone. Albany to Caiguna.
Shrub 0.2–1 m high. Six to ten hanging pink or white flowers 5–10 mm long in a head 10–20 mm across. Furry, oval to triangular leaves 1–6 cm long x 5–30 mm wide.

COAST VELVET BUSH
Lasiopetalum discolor

DATE	PLACE
10/97	Lake Grace

OCTOBER-JANUARY AND MARCH-APRIL
VERY COMMON

Woodland and heath in sand in wet areas. Jurien to Perth, Albany, Cape Le Grand and Southern Cross.
Shrub 1–2.5 m high. Globular pink to purple flowers 10–15 mm across at end of branches. Oval or triangular scale-like leaves 1–2 mm long x 1 mm wide closely pressed against stem.

SMALL REGELIA
Regelia inops

DATE	PLACE
10/92	Stirling Range National Park
10/05	Point Ann

HAIRY TRIGGERPLANT

Stylidium hirsutum

SEPTEMBER-DECEMBER
UNCOMMON

Heath in sand or clay. Narrogin to Denmark, Esperance and Jerramungup.
Slender plant 25–70 cm high. Very hairy pink or red flowers 10–15 mm long x 10 mm wide on hairy red stem 25–70 cm long in spike 1–2 cm long. Grass-like leaves 5–15 mm long x 0.5–1 mm wide, all at base of plant.

DATE	PLACE
10/96	Karlgarin

NEEDLE-LEAVED TRIGGERPLANT

Stylidium leptophyllum

AUGUST-NOVEMBER
UNCOMMON

Woodland and heath in sand or gravel. Kalbarri to Perth, Denmark, Ravensthorpe and Narembeen.
Slender plant on stilts 5–30 cm high. Hairy pink or yellow flowers 10–15 mm long x 5 mm wide on hairy red stem in spike 3–4 cm long. Pointed, grass-like leaves 10–35 mm long x 1 mm wide, all at base of plant.

DATE	PLACE
10/96	Esperance
10/05	Cape Le Grand

SEPTEMBER-DECEMBER
VERY COMMON

Woodland and heath in sand in wet areas. Donnybrook to Hopetoun, Cape Arid and Ravensthorpe.
Slender plant 10–40 cm high. Hairy pink or red flowers 20–30 mm long x 15 mm wide on hairy stem 10–40 cm long in spike 5 cm long. Grass-like leaves 5–25 mm long x 0.5–1 mm wide, all at base of plant.

CRAB CLAWS
Stylidium macranthum

DATE	PLACE
10/97	East Mount Barren

SEPTEMBER-NOVEMBER   COMMON

Woodland and heath in sand on coastal sand dunes and rocky slopes. Hopetoun to Caiguna.
Slender plant 25–60 cm high. Hairy pink flowers 15 mm long x 10 mm wide on very hairy stem 25–50 cm long in spike 10 cm long. Hairy, grass-like leaves 15–25 mm long x 1–4 mm wide, all at base of plant.

SILKY TRIGGERPLANT
Stylidium pilosum

DATE	PLACE
10/97	Corrigin

SPLENDID FEATHERFLOWER

Verticordia brachypoda

SEPTEMBER-DECEMBER
UNCOMMON

Forest and heath in sand or gravel. Mullewa to Eneabba, Borden, Ravensthorpe and Southern Cross. Shrub 0.1–1.5 m high. Pink, cream or white feathery flowers 10–15 mm across in umbrella-shaped head at end of branches. Oblong leaves 2–10 mm long x 0.5–1 mm wide, crowded on short side branches.

DATE	PLACE
10/92	Tarin Rock, Lake Grace

DAINTY FEATHERFLOWER

Verticordia inclusa

AUGUST-NOVEMBER
UNCOMMON

Woodland and heath in sand or gravel. Kellerberrin to Jerramungup, Wharton, Coolgardie and Koolyanobbing.
Shrub 0.1–2 m high. Pink or white feathery flowers 10 mm across. Spear-shaped to oval three-sided leaves 2–5 mm long x 2 mm wide.

DATE	PLACE
10/97	Lake Grace

AUGUST-DECEMBER
COMMON

STRIKING PINK FEATHERFLOWER
Verticordia insignis

Forest and heath in sand or gravel. Eneabba to Perth, Kojonup, Ongerup, Forrestania and Koorda. Shrub 0.2–1.5 m high. Pink to white feathery flowers 10–15 mm across on stalk 10–15 mm long in umbrella-shaped head at end of branches. Oval three-sided leaves 2–15 mm long x 2–5 mm wide.

DATE	PLACE
1/91	Fitzgerald River
	National Park

OCTOBER-JANUARY AND
MARCH TO JULY
COMMON

HOOK-LEAF FEATHERFLOWER
Verticordia pennigera

Heath in sand, clay or gravel. Shark Bay to Bunbury, Mount Barker, Cape Riche, Ravensthorpe and Kellerberrin.
Shrub 10–60 cm high. Pink feathery flowers 5–10mm across, usually in spike 15–35 mm long at end of branches. Hairy, pointed, oblong leaves 2–4 mm long x 0.5 mm wide, crowded on short side branches and hooked at end.

PAINTED FEATHERFLOWER
Verticordia picta

DATE	PLACE
10/95	Corrigin

JULY-DECEMBER
VERY COMMON

Heath in sand or clay. Kalbarri to Perth, Cranbrook, Bremer Bay, Salmon Gums and Coolgardie.
Shrub 0.3–1.5 m high. Pink to white feathery flowers 10 mm across in umbrella-shaped head at end of branches. Pointed, needle-like leaves 5–10 mm long x 0.5 mm wide.

LEAFLESS TETRATHECA
Tetratheca efoliata

DATE	PLACE
9/97	Newdegate

JULY-DECEMBER   UNCOMMON

Heath in sand or gravel. Beacon to Kellerberrin, Lake Grace, Norseman, Coolgardie and Koolyanobbing.
Shrub 10–40 cm high. Hanging pink flowers with purple centres 10–15 mm across on leafless stems.

DATE	PLACE
9/97	East Mount Barren

MAY-NOVEMBER   COMMON

Woodland and heath in sand. Corrigin to Kulin, and Mount Barker to Cape Riche and Munglinup.
Shrub 0.5–2 m high. Very woolly brown, yellow, cream or grey flowers (soft yellow-grey in bud) in a cylinder 5–15 cm long x 10–12 cm wide. Wedge-shaped, saw-toothed leaves 5–15 cm long x 1–4 cm wide.

WOOLLY BANKSIA
Banksia baueri

DATE	PLACE
10/97	Harrismith

AUGUST-MAY
VERY COMMON

VIOLET BANKSIA
Banksia violacea

Heath in sand. Brookton to Katanning, Ongerup, Esperance and Forrestania.
Shrub 0.2–2 m high. Globular brown to violet or purple and yellow or green flowers 6–8 cm round. Blunt, oblong leaves 10–25 mm long x 1–2 mm wide, curled under lengthwise.

DATE	PLACE
10/97	Tarin Rock, Lake Grace

AUGUST-OCTOBER   COMMON

Heath in gravel. Corrigin to Kukerin, Jerramungup, Lake King and Hyden.
Shrub 1–3 m high always leaning. Hairy, globular, red female flowers 5–10 mm across; brown male flowers in spikes 5–10 mm long x 2–5 mm wide on separate plant. Needle-like branches 20–45 mm long x 1 mm wide, ending in a sharp point. Cylindrical pine-like nut 20–25 mm long x 15–20 mm wide.

COMPASS BUSH
Allocasuarina pinaster

DATE	PLACE
9/97	Hamersley Drive

MAY-OCTOBER   UNCOMMON

Heath in sand or gravel. Harrismith to Bunbury, Margaret River, Hopetoun and Lake King.
Straggly or sprawling shrub 10–80 cm high. Orange and pink or red pea flowers 10 mm across in spike 2–10 cm long. Veined, oblong or oval leaves 15–75 mm long x 2–10 mm wide, ending in a sharp hooked point.

ORANGE FLAME PEA
Chorizema glycinifolium

DATE	PLACE
9/00	Hamersley Drive

AUGUST-JANUARY
COMMON

ORANGE RATTLE PEA
Daviesia alternifolia

Heath in sand or gravel. Nannup, and Denmark to Hopetoun, Ravensthorpe and Cranbrook.
Shrub 20–40 cm high. Groups of three orange and red pea flowers 10–15 mm across surrounded by three triangular leaf-like cups at end of branches. Oblong to spear-shaped leaves 1–5 cm long x 2–6 mm wide, hooked at end.

DATE	PLACE
9/97	East Mount Barren
10/05	Quaalup

JULY-DECEMBER   UNCOMMON

Heath in sand, clay or gravel. Two Peoples Bay, and Bremer Bay to Esperance, Ravensthorpe and Jerramungup.
Shrub 0.1–1 m high. Orange or yellow and red or brown pea flowers 5–7 mm across. Sharp, needle-like leaves 5–15 mm long x 1 mm wide, pointing down.

REVERSE-LEAF BITTER PEA
Daviesia incrassata subsp. *reversifolia*

PRICKLY PARROT PEA
Dillwinyia pungens

DATE	PLACE
9/00	East Mount Barren

AUGUST-NOVEMBER
UNCOMMON

Heath in sand on rocky slopes. Two Peoples Bay to Cape Arid.
Shrub 0.5–2 m high. Orange to yellow and red pea flowers 5–7 mm across in bunch at end of branches. Needle-like leaves 10–20 mm long x 1 mm wide, ending in a sharp point.

WHEEL SUNDEW
Drosera leucoblasta

DATE	PLACE
10/96	Esperance

AUGUST-NOVEMBER   COMMON

Forest, woodland and heath in gravelly sand or clay. Eneabba to Donnybrook, Albany, Wharton, Kellerberrin and Three Springs.
Herb 5–15 cm high. Orange, white, red or pink flowers 10–15 mm across at end of stalk 5–15 cm long. Sticky, hairy, round leaves 2–5 mm across on stalk 5–7 mm long, and silver hairs 3–5 mm long, in crowded wheel at base of plant.

41

DATE	PLACE
9/94	Dryandra

JULY-OCTOBER
VERY COMMON

GOLDEN DRYANDRA
Dryandra nobilis

Woodland in sand, clay or gravel. Eneabba to Wagin, Katanning and Dumbleyung. Shrub 0.5–4 m high. Orange to golden or yellow flowers in a head 7–10 cm across. Prickly, saw-toothed leaves 5–20 cm long x 5–15 mm wide.

DATE	PLACE
10/96	Corrigin

JULY-FEBRUARY
VERY COMMON

COMMON EREMAEA
Eremaea pauciflora

Woodland and heath in sand. Northampton to Dunsborough, Rocky Gully, Albany, Munglinup, Coolgardie and Merredin.
Shrub 0.3–2 m high. Orange flowers 5–10 mm across at end of branches. Smooth or hairy to woolly oblong leaves 5–15 mm long x 0.5–3 mm wide.

DATE	PLACE
9/97	*Ravensthorpe*

JUNE-NOVEMBER VERY COMMON

Woodland and heath in sand or gravel. Mullewa to Cataby, Mundaring, Cape Riche, Cape Arid and Coolgardie.
Shrub 0.2–2 m high. Orange or yellow and red pea flowers 5–10 mm across in spikes 2–5 cm long x 15 mm wide at end of stem. Silky, oblong to oval leaves 10–50 mm long x 5–15 mm wide, curled under lengthwise, with numerous cross-veins and ending in a slight depression or notch.

BOX POISON

Gastrolobium parviflorum

DATE	PLACE
9/00	*Quairading*

JULY-OCTOBER COMMON

Woodland and heath in sand. Coorow to Mundaring, Borden and Lake King.
Shrub 0.2–1 m high. Orange or yellow and red or pink pea flowers 5–8 mm across in spikes 2–4 cm long x 10–15 mm wide at end of stem. Oblong to elliptical blue-green leaves 5–10 mm long x 2–15 mm wide, with numerous cross-veins, ending in a slight depression or notch and hooked at end.

BERRY POISON

Gastrolobium parvifolium

DATE	PLACE
9/95	Bluff Knoll

MAY AND
AUGUST–JANUARY
VERY COMMON

PRICKLY POISON
Gastrolobium spinosum

Forest and woodland. Northampton to Dunsborough, Manjimup, Albany, Esperance, Widgiemooltha and Southern Cross.
Shrub 0.3–2 m high. Orange to yellow and red pea flowers 10–15 mm across in clusters along stem. Prickly, toothed, arrowhead-shaped leaves 1–4 cm long x 1–4 cm wide with five to eleven sharp points.

DATE	PLACE
10/95	Dryandra

SEPTEMBER–NOVEMBER   UNCOMMON

Woodland in sand. Three Springs to Coorow, and Williams to Katanning, Lake Grace and Kondinin.
Shrub 0.5–2.5 m high. Brown and white flowers (silky brown in bud) in groups 15–20 mm across along branch. Thick, prickly, toothed, fan-shaped leaves 3–6 cm long x 2–7 cm wide. Round, wrinkled, grooved, woody nut 3–5 cm long x 4–5 cm wide with small beak at end.

FAN HAKEA
Hakea brownii

44

DATE	PLACE
10/96	Karlgarin

SEPTEMBER-JANUARY   VERY COMMON

Heath often in disturbed areas. Morawa to Kukerin, Lake King, Salmon Gums and Southern Cross.
Shrub 0.5–2 m high. Brown to purple and yellow flowers in spikes 3–10 cm long x 15–20 mm wide at the end of long leafless stems. Wavy, bluey-green leaves 5–20 cm long near base of plant divided into oval or elliptical lobes 10–30 mm long x 10–20 mm wide, each ending in a sharp point.

CURLY GREVILLEA
Grevillea eryngioides

DATE	PLACE
10/95	Corrigin
10/05	Hyden

AUGUST-NOVEMBER
VERY COMMON

ORANGE FLAME GREVILLEA
Grevillea excelsior

Woodland and heath in sand or gravel. Mingenew to Dumbleyung, Salmon Gums, Coolgardie and Southern Cross.
Shrub or tree 1–8 m high. Orange to yellow flowers in spikes 5–20 cm long x 5 cm wide at the end of short leafless stems. Straight, pointed leaves 5–30 cm long often divided into many segments 10–20 cm long x 1 mm wide.

DATE	PLACE
8/96	Hyden

MAY-OCTOBER
COMMON

YORKRAKINE GREVILLEA

Grevillea yorkrakinensis

Woodland and heath in sand, clay or gravel, often near granite rocks. Morawa to Hyden, Boorabbin and Paynes Find.
Shrub 15–50 cm high. Furry orange or red and yellow flowers 15–25 mm long x 5 mm wide. Oblong leaves 5–15 mm long x 0.5–1 mm wide, ending in a sharp curved point.

DATE	PLACE
9/98	Fitzgerald River National Park
10/06	Two Peoples Bay

SEPTEMBER-NOVEMBER
COMMON

LEATHERY-LEAVED PEA

Nemcia coriacea

Woodland and heath on rock. Busselton to Pemberton, Albany, Hopetoun and Cranbrook.
Shrub 0.5–2.5 m high. Orange to yellow and red pea flowers (woolly brown and white in bud) 10 mm across in clusters 20–30 mm across. Oval to elliptical leaves 2–5 cm long x 10–25 mm wide, veined above and silky below, ending in a small point.

46

DATE	PLACE
10/97	Hyden

PINS AND NEEDLES
Stylidium dichotomum

SEPTEMBER-JANUARY
VERY COMMON

Woodland and heath. Kalbarri to Busselton, Denmark, Munglinup and Westonia.
Erect or creeping plant on stilts 5–40 cm high. Orange, yellow, pink or white hairy flowers 10–15 mm long and 5 mm wide on hairy red stem 5–35 cm long. Needle-like leaves 5–50 mm long x 0.5 mm wide, all at base of plant and ending in a sharp point.

DATE	PLACE
10/97	Harrismith

MOP BUSHPEA
Urodon dasyphyllus

JULY-DECEMBER
VERY COMMON

Woodland and heath in sand. Billabong to Northampton, and Wyalkatchem to York, Kulin, Munglinup and Coolgardie.
Shrub 10–60 cm high. Orange to yellow and red pea flowers (woolly greeny white in bud) 10 mm across in clusters 25–40 mm across at end of branches. Oval to elliptical, sometimes hairy, leaves 5–10 mm long x 1–3 mm wide, ending in a sharp point.

DATE	PLACE
9/00	Lucky Bay
10/05	Cape Le Grand

AUGUST-FEBRUARY　　　VERY COMMON

Heath in sand. Harvey to Augusta, Albany, Cape Arid, Mount Barker and Bridgetown.
Rush 0.4–1.5 m high. Long, thin, curved, yellow or red waxy female flowers 1–2 cm long x 2 mm wide in a spike 5–15 cm long x 2–3 cm wide; yellow to brown, fluffy male flowers in a spike 10–15 cm long x 3–5 cm wide on separate plants. Sword-shaped leaves 50–75 cm long x 5–10 mm wide, all at base of plant.

FLAT FLAG RUSH

Anarthria scabra

DATE	PLACE
8/96	Hyden

MAY-SEPTEMBER　　　UNCOMMON

Woodland and heath in sand. Carnamah to Lake Grace, Salmon Gums, Zanthus and Sandstone.
Herb in tufts 15–70 cm high. Masses of yellow or white star-shaped flowers 5 mm across in a spike 20 cm long x 5 mm wide at end of stalk 5–30 cm long. Grass-like leaves 20–60 cm long x 1–2 mm wide, all at base of plant.

SPREADING FRINGE LEAF

Chamaexeros fimbriata

RASPBERRY JAM
Acacia acuminata

DATE	PLACE
9/00	Brookton
09/07	*Salvallin*

AUGUST-OCTOBER   VERY COMMON

Woodland in gravel or clay. Kalbarri to Dongara, Wagin, Wellstead, Salmon Gums, Kalgoorlie and Mullewa.
Shrub or tree 1–12 m high. Numerous fluffy yellow flowers in a cylinder 1–4 cm long x 5 mm wide. Curved, oblong leaves 5–15 cm long x 1–5 mm wide, hooked at end.

SILVER WATTLE
Acacia lasiocalyx

DATE	PLACE
9/00	Kondinin

AUGUST-OCTOBER   VERY COMMON

Woodland in gravel or clay, mostly near granite rocks. Eneabba to York, Wellstead, Cape Arid, Kalgoorlie, Southern Cross and Wubin.
Shrub or tree 2–12 m high with white stems. Numerous fluffy yellow flowers in a cylinder 2–4 cm long x 8 mm wide. Curved, oblong leaves 15–30 cm long x 2–10 mm wide, hooked at end.

DATE	PLACE
9/00	Ravensthorpe

AUGUST-OCTOBER   COMMON

Woodland in sand, clay or rocky soil. Wellstead to Ravensthorpe.
Prostrate, spreading shrub 30–80 cm high. Fifteen to twenty fluffy yellow flowers in a ball 4–5 mm round on stalks 5 mm long. Flat, winged stems becoming leaves 1–3 cm long x 5–15 mm wide, each ending in a sharp point.

SMALL FLAT WATTLE

Acacia bifaria

DATE	PLACE
9/00	John Forrest Track
10/05	Hamersley Drive

AUGUST-OCTOBER   COMMON

Heath in clay or gravel. Wagin to Albany, Cape Arid and Newdegate.
Prostrate or upright, usually sprawling shrub 0.3–1.5 m high. Thirty to eighty fluffy yellow flowers in a ball 5–7 mm round on stalks 1–3 mm long. Flat, winged stems becoming leaves 2–7 cm long x 5–20 mm wide, each ending in a sharp point.

FLAT WATTLE

Acacia glaucoptera

DATE	PLACE
9/00	Ravensthorpe

HEDGEHOG WATTLE
Acacia erinacea

JUNE-DECEMBER
VERY COMMON

Woodland and heath. Kalbarri to Eneabba, Borden, Eucla and Menzies.
Shrub 0.1–1.5 m high with many spines 5–7 mm long. Ten to twenty fluffy golden flowers in a ball 3–5 mm round on reddish stalks. Spear-shaped leaves 5–20 mm long x 2–4 mm wide, ending in a sharp point.

DATE	PLACE
9/00	Quairading

JULY-SEPTEMBER   VERY COMMON

Woodland in sand. Kalbarri to Jurien, Armadale, Cranbrook, Salmon Gums, Coolgardie and Yalgoo.
Shrub 0.2–2.5 m high forming a dome. Numerous fluffy, yellow flowers in a cylinder 10–25 mm long x 5 mm wide. Sharp, pointed, flat or needle-like leaves 2–10 cm long x 1–2 mm wide, with ten to twenty veins and often hooked at end.

DOME WATTLE
Acacia multispicata

DATE	PLACE
9/00	Cape Le Grand

JUNE-NOVEMBER   COMMON

Woodland and heath in sand, often on sand dunes or granite rocks. Hopetoun, and Esperance to Cape Arid.
Shrub 0.4–2 m high, sometimes with hairy stem. Numerous fluffy yellow flowers in a ball 3–5 mm round in groups of two to six. Two to eight pairs of soft or spiny oval leaflets 3–8 mm long x 2–4 mm wide along leaf.

ESPERANCE WATTLE

Acacia nigricans

DATE	PLACE
8/96	Hyden

AUGUST-SEPTEMBER
UNCOMMON

TRIANGLE-LEAVED WATTLE

Acacia trigonophylla

Woodland in sand or gravel. Geraldton to Mingenew, and Armadale to Busselton, Windy Harbour, Hyden and Mukinbudin.
Shrub 1–2.5 m high. Numerous fluffy yellow flowers in a ball 5–7 mm round. Flat, curved leaves 5–40 mm long x 1–2 mm wide, ending in a sharp point and becoming wings along stem.

DATE	PLACE
1/91	Hamersley Inlet

JULY-OCTOBER AND JANUARY-MARCH
COMMON

Woodland in sand. Cranbrook to Cheyne Beach and Munglinup.
Shrub or tree 2–4 m high. Yellow to greenish-yellow egg-shaped flowers 5–8 cm long x 3–7 cm wide. Prickly, saw-toothed leaves 10–20 cm long x 2–8 cm wide.

BAXTER'S BANKSIA
Banksia baxteri

DATE	PLACE
9/00	Cape Le Grand
10/05	Cape Le Grand

MAY-FEBRUARY   VERY COMMON

Woodland and heath in sand. Hopetoun to Cape Arid and Salmon Gums.
Shrub or tree 1–8 m high. Yellow to greenish-yellow flowers in a cylinder 5–15 cm long x 10 cm wide. Prickly, saw-toothed leaves 20–45 cm long x 2–4 cm wide.

SHOWY BANKSIA
Banksia speciosa

DATE	PLACE
10/95	*John Forrest Track*
10/05	East Mount Barren

SEPTEMBER-MARCH   COMMON

Woodland in rocky soil. Borden to Wellstead, Munglinup and Ravensthorpe.
Shrub 1–5 m high. Hanging yellow to green flowers in a cylinder 5–10 cm long x 8–10 cm wide. Wavy, prickly, saw-toothed leaves 3–10 cm long x 1–4 cm wide.

LEMANN'S BANKSIA
Banksia lemanniana

DATE	PLACE
9/97	*Ravensthorpe*

SEPTEMBER-JANUARY
UNCOMMON

TENNIS BALL BANKSIA
Banksia laevigata

Woodland on hilltops. Southern Cross to Hyden, Lake King, Ongerup, Esperance and Salmon Gums.
Shrub or tree 1–3.5 m high. Globular, yellow to greenish-yellow and grey flowers (woolly brown in bud) 5–8 cm across. Prickly, saw-toothed leaves 5–15 cm long x 5–20 mm wide.

SOUTHERN PLAINS BANKSIA
Banksia media

DATE	PLACE
9/00	Moir Track

AUGUST-OCTOBER AND FEBRUARY-JUNE
VERY COMMON

Woodland and heath in sand or clay. Lake King to Wellstead, Cape Riche, Caiguna and Salmon Gums.
Shrub 0.5–5 m high. Yellow or yellow and brown flowers in a cylinder 5–15 cm long x 5–8 cm wide. Prickly, saw-toothed leaves 5–15 cm long x 5–20 mm wide.

TEASELBANKSIA
Banksia pulchella

DATE	PLACE
9/00	Scaddan
10/05	Cape Le Grand

MARCH-OCTOBER   UNCOMMON

Woodland and heath in sand. Ravensthorpe to Hopetoun and Cape Arid.
Shrub 0.2–1.5 m high. Globular to cylindrical yellow to orange and brown flowers 2–5 cm long x 3–5 cm wide. Oblong leaves 5–15 mm long x 1 mm wide.

DATE	PLACE
9/97	Mylies Beach
10/05	Quaalup

SEPTEMBER-APRIL   VERY COMMON

Heath in sand or gravel. Busselton to Augusta and Bridgetown, and Walpole to Cape Arid and Jerramungup.
Shrub 0.5–2 m high. Cream to white flowers in spikes 25–45 mm long x 15–30 mm wide at the end of leafless stems 0.3–1 m long. Pointed rush-like leaves 15–40 cm long x 1 mm wide, all at base of plant.

SPIDER SMOKEBUSH
Conospermum teretifolium

DATE	PLACE
9/00	Cape Le Grand
10/05	Quaalup

AUGUST-NOVEMBER   COMMON

Heath and sand dunes in sand. Cranbrook to Albany, Cape Arid and Ravensthorpe.
Straggly and spindly shrub 0.1–1 m high. Globular yellow flowers 7–10 mm across. Soft, sometimes silky, oval leaves 1–5 mm long x 1–2 mm wide.

GOLDEN CONEBUSH
Conothamnus aureus

SANDPLAIN COTTONHEADS
Conostylis petrophiloides

DATE	PLACE
10/98	John Forrest Track

AUGUST–DECEMBER
UNCOMMON

Heath in sand. Wyalkatchem to Boddington, Hopetoun and Forrestania, and Cranbrook.
Herb in tufts 15-30 cm high. Numerous woolly yellow flowers in globular heads 2–4 cm across on woolly stems 5–10 cm long. Flat, sword-shaped leaves 5–20 cm long x 1–4 mm wide, hairy on edge and all at base of plant.

STARBURST COTTONHEADS
Conostylis phathyrantha

DATE	PLACE
9/00	Scaddan
10/05	Esperance

JULY–OCTOBER   UNCOMMON

Heath in sand. Munglinup to Cape Arid and Salmon Gums.
Herb in tufts 15–30 cm high. Woolly yellow and white tubular flowers 10–15 mm long x 5–20 mm wide on woolly stems 3–10 cm long. Flat, sword-shaped leaves 10–30 cm long x 2–5 mm wide, woolly on edge and all at base of plant.

57

DATE	PLACE
9/97	East Mount Barren
10/05	Quaalup

AUGUST–NOVEMBER
COMMON

SHEATH COTTONHEADS
Conostylis vaginata

Heath in sand or clay. Cranbrook to Cape Riche, Munglinup and Salmon Gums. Herb in tufts on stilts 5–30 cm high. Four to six bristly, woolly yellow flowers 2 cm long x 15–25 mm wide in group at base of plant. Flat or needle-like leaves 5–10 cm long x 0.5–1 mm wide, all at base of plant.

DATE	PLACE
9/00	Moir Track

JULY-OCTOBER
COMMON

OUCH BUSH
Daviesia pachyphylla

Heath in sand or gravel. Newdegate to Cape Riche, Munglinup and Lake King. Straggly shrub 0.3–1.5 m high. Groups of three to six yellow to orange and red or brown pea flowers 3–5 mm across. Thick, stumpy leaves 10–20 mm long x 3–6 mm wide, ending in a sharp point.

DATE	PLACE
10/96	Munglinup
10/05	Esperance, Woody Lake

SEPTEMBER-NOVEMBER   UNCOMMON

Woodland and wet areas. Bremer Bay to Cape Arid.
Slender plant 20–40 cm high. One to five yellow and brown flowers 3 cm long x 2–3 cm wide. Grass-like leaves 10–15 cm long x 1–2 mm wide at base of plant.

ELEGANT DONKEY ORCHID
Diuris concinna

DATE	PLACE
9/98	Esperance

AUGUST-OCTOBER
VERY COMMON

BEE ORCHID
Diuris laxiflora

Woodland and heath in wet areas. Mullewa to Geraldton, Augusta, Cape Arid and Kellerberrin.
Slender plant 10–30 cm high. One to five yellow and brown flowers 1–2 cm long x 1–2 cm wide. Grass-like leaves 5–15 cm long x 3 mm wide at base of plant.

DATE	PLACE
9/92	Narrogin
10/05	Corrigin

AUGUST-DECEMBER
VERY COMMON

SUNNY RAINBOW
Drosera subhirtella

Woodland and heath in moist areas. Carnamah to Jurien, Bunbury, Albany, Lake King and Mukinbudin.
Climbing plant 10–40 cm high. Yellow flowers (black in bud) 15–20 mm across. Sticky, hairy, round leaves 2–5 mm across in groups of three (on one 5 cm long and two 3–5 mm long stalks) on stem.

DATE	PLACE
10/98	Mount Desmond, Ravensthorpe
10/05	Mason Bay

AUGUST-DECEMBER
VERY COMMON

BELL-FRUITED MALLEE
Eucalyptus preissiana

Woodland. Cranbrook to Cheyne Beach, Esperance and Ravensthorpe.
Straggly tree 2–3 m high. Yellow flowers 2–3 cm across with red cap before flowering. Thick, flat, oval leaves 5–12 cm long x 2–4 cm wide.

RUSTY DRYANDRA
Dryandra ferruginea

DATE	PLACE
9/92	Tarin Rock, Lake Grace

JULY-NOVEMBER
COMMON

Heath in clay or gravel. Quairading to Cranbrook, Ravensthorpe, Forrestania and Bruce Rock.
Sprawling shrub 0.2–1.5 m high. Yellow flowers surrounded by yellow leaf-like lobes with orange to brown tips in a head 5–8 cm across hidden in leaves. Wavy, prickly, saw-toothed leaves 15–30 cm long x 1–2 cm wide on stem 10–20 cm long.

SHINING HONEYPOT
Dryandra obtusa

DATE	PLACE
9/97	Mylies Beach

AUGUST-NOVEMBER   UNCOMMON

Heath in sand. Jerramungup to Cape Arid and Scaddan.
Sprawling prostrate shrub 10–20 cm high. Yellow and brown flowers in a head 4–5 cm long x 3–5 cm wide coming out of ground. Saw-toothed leaves 15–30 cm long x 10–15 mm wide.

DATE	PLACE
9/97	East Mount Barren

JULY-OCTOBER AND FEBRUARY-MARCH
VERY COMMON

Heath in sand or on rocky hillsides. Bremer Bay to Hopetoun and Ravensthorpe.
Shrub 1–3 m high. Yellow, green and orange to brown flowers in a head 3–8 cm across. Prickly, wedge-shaped or oblong leaves 2–10 cm long x 1–4 cm wide.

OAK-LEAVED DRYANDRA
Dryandra quercifolia

DATE	PLACE
9/00	Cape Le Grand

JULY-SEPTEMBER AND
MARCH-APRIL
VERY COMMON

COMMON POPFLOWER
Glischrocaryon aureum

Woodland and heath. Shark Bay to Augusta, Caiguna and Giles.
Shrub 0.2–1m high. Yellow flowers 10 mm across in umbrella-shaped head 2–7 cm across which swell up into a ball and pop open. Straight leaves 0.5–6 cm long x 0.5–4 mm wide.

DATE	PLACE
9/92	Yillimilling Rock, Narrogin

BLACK AND GOLD PEA
Gompholobium marginatum

AUGUST-NOVEMBER
UNCOMMON

Forest, woodland and heath in gravel and granite. Geraldton, Jurien, and Gingin to Perth, Augusta, Cape Arid and Harrismith.
Shrub 10–40 cm high. Yellow pea flowers 10 mm across. Oval to spear-shaped leaves 10–20 mm long x 5–10 mm wide, in threes, with a thick margin and ending in a sharp point.

DATE	PLACE
10/95	Ravensthorpe

NEEDLE TREE
Hakea preissii

AUGUST-DECEMBER
COMMON

Woodland in sand or clay. Onslow to Northampton, Kojonup, Bremer Bay, Cape Arid, Wiluna and Paraburdoo, and Busselton to Margaret River.
Shrub or tree 1–6 m high. Four to twenty eight yellow or green and red to pink flowers in clusters 15–25 mm across. Needle-like leaves 1–6 cm long x 1–3 mm wide, ending in a sharp point. Oval, woody nut 15–25 mm long x 10 mm wide with two horns.

DATE	PLACE
9/86	West River, Jerramungup

JUNE-NOVEMBER
COMMON

SILVER GOODENIA

Goodenia affinis

Heath in sand or clay. Moora to Cape Riche, Cocklebiddy, Forrestania and Mukinbudin. Circular, domed, cushion shrub 5–50 cm high. Yellow flowers 10–20 mm across. Wavy, woolly, spoon-shaped, sometimes toothed, leaves 2–10 cm long x 2–20 mm wide.

DATE	PLACE
9/00	Ravensthorpe

AUGUST-DECEMBER
UNCOMMON

SMOOTH GOODENIA

Goodenia laevis

Woodland in sand, clay or gravel. Kukerin to Jerramungup, Hopetoun, Cape Arid and Norseman.
Circular, spreading, prostrate shrub 2–25 cm high. Yellow flowers 10–15 mm across. Spear- or spoon-shaped leaves 1–3 cm long x 1–8 mm wide.

CUSHION GUINEA FLOWER
Hibbertia enervia

DATE	PLACE
9/94	Dryandra

APRIL-FEBRUARY
COMMON

Woodland in sand or gravel. Jurien to Busselton, Denmark, Esperance and Southern Cross.
Erect or spreading, prostrate shrub 5–60 cm high. Yellow flowers 10 mm across. Crowded, blunt, needle-like leaves 5–10 mm long x 0.5–1 mm wide.

PRICKLY HIBBERTIA
Hibbertia mucronata

DATE	PLACE
10/96	Ravensthorpe

AUGUST-JANUARY AND MARCH-MAY
UNCOMMON

Woodland in sand on rocky hillsides. Jerramungup to Bremer Bay, Hopetoun and Ravensthorpe.
Rigid shrub 0.5–1 m high. Yellow flowers (hairy in bud) 10–15 mm across. Crowded, straight, rough (hairy when new) leaves 10–20 mm long x 1 mm wide, curled under lengthwise and ending in a sharp point.

DATE	PLACE
9/97	East Mount Barren
10/05	East Mount Barren

SEPTEMBER-JANUARY   COMMON

Heath in sand or gravel. Cranbrook to Mount Barker, Wellstead, Cape Arid and Ravensthorpe.
Shrub 0.3–2 m high. Yellow to greenish-yellow egg- to barrel-shaped flowers 2–5 cm long x 2–5 cm wide at top of stem. Thick wedge- or fan-shaped leaves 5–15 cm long x 1–4 cm wide, with 3–5 lobes or fingers at the top.

BARREL CONEFLOWER
Isopogon trilobus

DATE	PLACE
10/97	Tarin Rock, Lake Grace

SEPTEMBER-DECEMBER
UNCOMMON

WOOLLY CONEFLOWER
Isopogon villosus

Heath in sand or gravel. Brookton to Munglinup and Forrestania, and Cranbrook. Shrub 20–80 cm high. Woolly yellow flowers in globular heads 3–4 cm across, at base of plant. Forked leaves 5–80 cm long on long stalks divided at the end into many sharp, pointed, needle-like sections 2–15 mm long x 1 mm wide.

LEMON HONEYMYRTLE
Melaleuca citrina

DATE	PLACE
9/00	East Mount Barren
10/05	East Mt Barren

SEPTEMBER-NOVEMBER
COMMON

Heath in sand on rocky slopes. Jerramungup to Bremer Bay and Hopetoun.
Shrub 0.5–3 m high. Yellow flowers in a cylinder 10–25 mm long x 10–15 mm wide.
Spear-shaped leaves 5–15 mm long x 0.5–2 mm wide.

NEEDLE-LEAVED HONEYMYRTLE
Melaleuca pungens

DATE	PLACE
9/92	Tarin Rock, Lake Grace

JULY-DECEMBER
VERY COMMON

Heath in sand or gravel. Shark Bay, Northampton, and Eneabba to Mount Barker, Bremer Bay, Scaddan and Merredin.
Shrub 0.5–3.5 m high. Yellow flowers in a cylinder 10–15 mm long x 10 mm wide at end of branches. Needle-like leaves 1–3 cm long x 1 mm wide, ending in a sharp point.

DATE	PLACE
10/97	Harrismith

AUGUST-NOVEMBER
UNCOMMON

HOLLY-LEAVED HONEYSUCKLE

Lambertia ilicifolia

Heath in sand or gravel. Quairading to Williams, Kojonup and Newdegate. Shrub 0.2–2 m high. Group of seven to nine yellow tubular flowers 10–15 mm long x 3 mm wide in a head 10–15 mm across at end of branches. Folded, spear-shaped leaves 10–25 mm long x 5–10 mm wide in groups of three, curled backwards and ending in a sharp point.

DATE	PLACE
9/98	Point Ann, Bremer Bay
10/05	Quaalup

JULY-DECEMBER
COMMON

LONG-LEAVED PETROPHILE

Petrophile longifolia

Forest and heath. Williams to Walpole, Hopetoun, Lake King and Borden, and Augusta. Prostrate shrub 15–50 cm high. Yellow to white flowers in globular heads 4–5 cm long x 4–10 cm across, at base of plant. Needle-like leaves 5–30 cm long x 0.5–2 mm wide, all at base of plant.

NEEDLE-LEAVED PETROPHILE
Petrophile brevifolia

DATE	PLACE
10/97	Lake Grace
10/05	Corrigin

JUNE-DECEMBER
COMMON

Heath in sand. Shark Bay to Perth, Wagin, Borden, Ravensthorpe and Wongan Hills. Shrub 0.2–1 m high. Fluffy yellow flowers in globular heads 15–25 mm long x 2–4 cm across at tops of branches. Needle-like leaves 2–7 cm long x 1 mm wide, ending in a sharp point.

FINE-LEAVED PETROPHILE
Petrophile ericifolia

DATE	PLACE
9/92	Tarin Rock, Lake Grace
10/05	Corrigin

AUGUST-NOVEMBER
COMMON

Heath in sand or gravel. Kalbarri to Northam, Cranbrook, Cape Riche, Bremer Bay, Lake King and Morawa.
Shrub 0.2–1 m high. Sticky, fluffy yellow flowers in globular heads 2–3 cm across at tops of branches. Blunt, needle-like leaves 2–7 mm long x 0.5–1 mm wide.

DATE	PLACE
10/98	Mount Desmond, Ravensthorpe
10/05	Hamersley Drive

SEPTEMBER-NOVEMBER   COMMON

Heath in sand or gravel. Ravensthorpe to Hopetoun and Cape Arid.
Shrub 0.3–1.5 m high. Yellow flowers in cylindrical heads 2–10 cm long x 2 cm wide at tops of branches. Spreading, forked leaves 5–10 cm long on long stalks divided into many straight sections 5–20 mm long x 0.5–1 mm wide.

PINEAPPLE PETROPHILE
Petrophile fastigiata

DATE	PLACE
10/98	Mount Desmond, Ravensthorpe

AUGUST-NOVEMBER
COMMON

BLUE-LEAVED PETROPHILE
Petrophile glauca

Heath in sand or gravel. Narembeen to Corrigin, Wagin, Hopetoun and 100 mile Tank. Shrub 0.3–1.2 m high. Yellow flowers in globular heads 15–50 mm across at tops of branches. Spreading, prickly, forked, bluey-green leaves 5–15 cm long on long stalks divided into many straight sections 2–30 mm long x 1–5 mm wide, each ending in a sharp point.

GROOVED-LEAF SNOTTYGOBBLE
Persoonia saundersiana

DATE	PLACE
10/97	Karlgarin

AUGUST-NOVEMBER
COMMON

Woodland and heath in sand. Geraldton to Cranbrook, Salmon Gums, Menzies and Beacon, and Cue.
Shrub 0.5–5 m high. Several swollen, smooth or rough, tubular yellow flowers 15–20 mm long x 5 mm wide in a group. Curved, flat, grooved, oblong leaves 5–15 cm long x 1–3 mm wide.

NEEDLE-LEAVED SNOTTYGOBBLE
Persoonia teretifolia

DATE	PLACE
1/94	Kalgan River

SEPTEMBER-MAY   UNCOMMON

Woodland and heath in sand or clay. Kukerin to Albany, Cape Arid and 100 mile Tank, and Southern Cross.
Shrub 0.5–3 m high. Swollen, furry, tubular yellow flowers 10 mm long x 5 mm wide. Pointed, needle-like leaves 3–5 cm long x 1 mm wide.

DATE	PLACE
9/00	*Karlgarin*

JULY-NOVEMBER
COMMON

SLENDER PHEBALIUM
Phebalium filifolium

Woodland in sand or gravel. Koorda to Williams, Gnowangerup, Cape Arid and Menzies. Shrub 0.3–1.5 m high. Yellow or white flowers 5–8 mm across in groups 1–3 cm across at ends of branches. Warty, straight, silvery green and brown, aromatic leaves 5–20 mm long and 0.5–1 mm wide.

DATE	PLACE
10/96	*Karlgarin*

AUGUST-NOVEMBER
UNCOMMON

NERVED BUSH PEA
Pultenaea neurocalyx

Heath in sand or clay. Kellerberrin to Albany, Cape Arid and Koolyanobbing. Shrub 0.2–1.2 cm high. Yellow and red to purple pea flowers 5–10 mm across surrounded by grooved, hairy, spear-shaped leaf-like lobes 3–5 mm long x 1 mm wide. Oval scale-like leaves 1–10 mm long x 0.5–1 mm wide closely pressed against stem.

DATE	PLACE
10/97	Lake Grace

PROSTRATE GLOBE PEA

Sphaerolobium linophyllum

OCTOBER-FEBRUARY
UNCOMMON

Heath in sand or gravel. Carnamah to Lancelin, Augusta, Cape Arid and Merredin. Circular, spreading, prostrate shrub 5–40 cm high. Yellow to orange and red pea flowers 5–10 mm across. Straight leaves 5–10 mm long x 0.5 mm wide.

DATE	PLACE
10/96	Karlgarin

BOOMERANG TRIGGERPLANT

Stylidium breviscapum

SEPTEMBER-JANUARY
UNCOMMON

Forest, woodland and heath in sand or gravel. Northam to Dunsborough, Denmark, Cape Arid and Merredin.
Slender plant on stilts 5–20 cm high. Yellow or white and red flowers 5–10 mm long x 5 mm wide on hairy stem 5–20 mm long. Blunt, needle-like leaves 5–15 mm long x 0.5–1mm wide in a ring around middle of stem.

DATE	PLACE
10/95	East Mount Barren
10/05	East Mount Barren

SEPTEMBER-JANUARY UNCOMMON

Heath on rocky hillsides. Hopetoun.
Slender plant on stilts 10–50 cm high. Yellow or white flowers 10–20 mm long x 10 mm wide. Pointed, spear-shaped leaves 10–40 mm long x 5–10 mm wide in rings of six to nine around stem.

YELLOW MOUNTAIN TRIGGERPLANT
Stylidium galioides

DATE	PLACE
10/96	Karlgarin

SEPTEMBER-NOVEMBER,
APRIL AND JULY
COMMON

MAIZE TRIGGERPLANT
Stylidium squamellosum

Forest, woodland and heath. Morawa, and Calingiri to Pinjarra, Albany, Bremer Bay and 100 mile Tank.
Slender plant 5–35 cm high. Yellow to white flowers (purple on back) 5–15 mm long x 5 mm wide on stem 5–20 mm long in a spike 5–10 cm long. Pointed, spiny, grass-like leaves 15–40 mm long x 1–2 mm wide, all at base of plant.

GOLDEN FEATHERFLOWER
Verticordia chrysanthella

DATE	PLACE
10/97	Hyden

JULY-DECEMBER
VERY COMMON

Heath in sand or clay. Northampton to Lancelin, Kellerberrin, Albany, Lake Grace, Hopetoun, Munglinup and Mukinbudin.
Shrub 0.2–1 m high. Round yellow feathery flowers 5–8 mm across in umbrella-shaped head on stalk 5-15 mm long at end of branches. Blunt, warty, needle-like leaves 2–8 mm long x 0.5 mm wide, with a small hook at the end.

VILLARSIA
Villarsia parnassifolia

DATE	PLACE
10/96	Esperance

SEPTEMBER-MARCH AND JULY
VERY COMMON

Swamps and wet areas. Pinjarra to Dunsborough, Augusta, Cape Arid, Cranbrook and Manjimup.
Herb 0.1–1 m high. Woolly yellow flowers 10–20 mm across at end of stalk 0.1–1 m long in a spike 30–50 cm long. Toothed, circular or oval leaves 1–6 cm long x 1–4 cm wide, all at base of plant on stalk 3–20 cm long.

DATE	PLACE
10/95	East Mount Barren

JULY-DECEMBER   UNCOMMON

Heath on rocky slopes. Jerramungup to Bremer Bay and Hopetoun.
Shrub 0.5–1 m high. Several fluffy, creamy-white flowers in a ball 5 mm round. Straight, five-sided leaves 1–3 cm long x 1 mm wide, ending in a sharp point, in rings of about eight around stem.

BARRENS WATTLE

Acacia cedroides

DATE	PLACE
10/98	Mount Desmond, Ravensthorpe
10/05	Quaalup

JULY-NOVEMBER
COMMON

SPOON-LEAVED PEPPERMINT

Agonis spathulata

Heath in sand or rock. Cranbrook to Albany, Cape Arid and Lake King.
Shrub 0.2–2.5 m high. White flowers 10 mm across in dense bunches of up to twenty flowers at the end of stem. Thick, waxy, round to spoon-shaped leaves 3–7 mm across, often in rings of three around stem.

MOUNTAIN TAILFLOWER
Anthocercis fasciculata

DATE	PLACE
10/95	East Mount Barren

JULY-DECEMBER
UNCOMMON

Woodland and heath in sand on quartzite mountains near the coast. Bremer Bay to Hopetoun and Ravensthorpe.
Shrub 1–3.5 m high. Tubular white flowers 10–15 mm long x 15–20 mm across on hairy stalk 3–10 mm long. Spear-shaped leaves 1–4 cm long x 2–10 mm wide.

OVAL-LEAVED MYRTLE
Baeckea ovalifolia

DATE	PLACE
9/97	East Mount Barren
10/05	East Mount Barren

MAY AND AUGUST-NOVEMBER
COMMON

Heath in rocky soil. Quairading, and Ravensthorpe to Hopetoun.
Shrub 0.4–2 m high. Wavy white flowers (pink in bud) 10–15 mm across. Crowded, toothed, oval leaves 3 mm long x 2 mm wide.

DATE	PLACE
9/00	*Ravensthorpe*

FEBRUARY-NOVEMBER   UNCOMMON

Woodland in clay or gravel. Wongan Hills to Albany, Cape Arid, Salmon Gums and Newdegate, and Koolyanobbing and Menzies.
Climbing vine 1–4 m high with red stems. White tubular flowers 10–15 mm long x 5–10 mm wide turning purple. Shiny, oblong or spear-shaped leaves 10–40 mm long x 1–10 mm wide.

BELL CREEPER
Billardiera coriacea

DATE	PLACE
9/92	*Boyagin Rock*
08/06	Gt N Highway (N. of Bindoon)

AUGUST-SEPTEMBER
VERY COMMON

SUGAR ORCHID
Caladenia saccharata

Woodland and sheoak forests. Paynes Find to Bullsbrook, Kojonup, Cape Arid and Kalgoorlie.
Slender plant 5–15 cm high. One to two white flowers 2–3 cm across. Hairy grass-like leaf 5–10 cm long x 3 mm wide at base of plant.

DATE	PLACE
9/00	Hamersley Drive
10/05	Duaalup

LARGE WAXFLOWER
Chamelaucium megalopetalum

AUGUST-DECEMBER
VERY COMMON

Woodland and heath in sand or gravel. Harrismith to Bremer Bay, Cape Arid and Koolyanobbing.
Shrub 0.2–1.4 m high. White flowers 10-20 mm across turning pink, red or purple in head 3–5 cm across at end of branch. Straight leaves 3–6 mm long x 1–2 mm wide.

DATE	PLACE
10/96	Karlgarin

BLUE-EYED SMOKEBUSH
Conospermum brownii

SEPTEMBER-DECEMBER
UNCOMMON

Woodland and heath in sand. Perenjori to Wongan Hills, Ravensthorpe, Salmon Gums, Boorabbin and Kellerberrin.
Shrub 0.2–1.2 m high. White flowers with blue to purple centres in circular heads 3–8 cm across at the end of leafless stems 0.1–1 m long. Flat, spoon-shaped leaves 2–5 cm long and 5–10 mm wide, mostly near base of plant.

DATE	PLACE
9/97	Mylies Beach
10/05	Cape Le Grand NP

AUGUST-DECEMBER   VERY COMMON

Heath in sand or sandy gravel. Dumbleyung to Lake King, and Bremer Bay to Cape Arid.
Shrub 0.3–1.3 m high. Woolly white flowers with blue tips and greyish-blue tinge forming feather-duster-shaped heads 3–8 cm long x 2–4 cm across at the end of branches. Blunt, incurved, needle-like leaves 2–7 cm long x 0.5–1 mm wide.

FINE-LEAF SMOKEBUSH
Conospermum distichum

DATE	PLACE
9/92	Lake Grace

JULY-OCTOBER   COMMON

Heath in sand and gravel. Calingiri to York, Kukerin, Lake King and Wongan Hills.
Shrub 0.3–1 m high. White flowers with bluish or pinkish tinge 5 mm long in groups 10–15 mm across along most of the stem. Reed-like leaves 10–15 cm long x 1 mm wide, all at base of plant.

CRAB SMOKEBUSH
Conospermum ephedroides

DATE	PLACE
1/91	Fitzgerald River National Park

JANUARY-DECEMBER   UNCOMMON

Woodland in clay in wet areas and along rivers. Telfer to Carnarvon, Busselton, Bremer Bay, Eucla and Warburton.
Hairy prostrate or climbing vine 1–2 m long. White or pink tubular flowers 10–30 mm across on stalk 3–6 cm long. Crinkled, hairy, oval to triangular leaves 10–40 mm long x 5–30 mm wide on stalks 1–2 cm long and often divided into three to seven triangular or oblong fingers.

AUSTRALIAN BINDWEED

Convolvulus erubescens

DATE	PLACE
9/00	Corrigin

MAY-JANUARY   COMMON

Woodland and heath in sand or gravel. Kalbarri to Perth, Manjimup, Albany, Cape Arid and Merredin.
Shrub 0.2–1 m high with many spiny branches 7–10 mm long. Crowded, white tubular flowers (hairy in bud) 3–5 mm long x 2–3 mm across. Oblong to oval leaves 2–6 mm long x 0.5–1 mm wide, curled under lengthwise, rough above and hairy below.

SPINY CRYPTANDRA

Cryptandra pungens

DATE	PLACE
12/90	Qualup

SEPTEMBER-FEBRUARY
VERY COMMON

TALLARACK
Eucalyptus pleurocarpa

Heath in sand. Eneabba, and Forrestania to Cranbrook, Albany, Wharton and 100 Mile Tank.
Straggly shrub or tree 1–8 m high with white 4-winged branches. White to cream flowers 2–3 cm across in groups of three on 4-winged stem. Thick, blue-green, oval leaves (silver or white when new) 7–15 cm long x 3–5 cm wide.

DATE	PLACE
10/97	Lake Grace

AUGUST-JANUARY
UNCOMMON

PALLURUP GREVILLEA
Grevillea prostrata

Heath in sand or gravel. Lake Grace to Jerramungup, Lake King and Hyden.
Prostrate shrub 5–10 mm high. White to pink flowers with rotten meat odour 2 cm across. Leaves 2–7 cm long x 1–4 cm wide, divided into nine to thirteen straight lobes 0.5–40 mm long x 1–2 mm wide, each curled under lengthwise and ending in a sharp point.

SWAN FRUIT HAKEA
Hakea cygna

DATE	PLACE
8/96	*Corrigin*

MAY-SEPTEMBER   VERY COMMON

Woodland or heath in sand or gravel. Northampton to Narrogin, Bremer Bay, Cape Arid and Forrestania.
Shrub 0.5–2 m high. White flowers 7 mm long in clusters 10 mm across along branch. Thick, oblong leaves 2–8 cm long x 1–10 mm wide, ending in a sharp point. Flat, oval, woody nut 2–4 cm long x 15–25 mm wide with short beak at end.

RUSTY HAKEA
Hakea ferruginea

DATE	PLACE
9/00	Hamersley Drive
10/05	*Hamersley Drive*

JULY-NOVEMBER   VERY COMMON

Forest or woodland in sand or gravel. Mount Barker to Albany and Esperance. Shrub 1–2 m high. White flowers 6–10 mm long in clusters 10–15 mm across in cup of leaves along branch. Oval to heart-shaped leaves 2–8 cm long x 10–25 mm wide (brown when new) ending in a sharp point. Oval, woody nut 2–3 cm long x 1–2 cm wide with long beak at end.

DATE	PLACE
9/00	Kwolyin

AUGUST-SEPTEMBER
VERY COMMON

GILBERT'S HAKEA

Hakea gilbertii

Heath. Eneabba to Katanning, Corrigin and Wongan Hills.
Shrub 0.5–1.5 m high. White or pinkish flowers 10 mm long in dense clusters 10–20 mm across. Needle-like leaves 2–10 cm long x 1 mm wide ending in a very long sharp point. Warty, oval, woody nut 10–15 mm long x 10 mm wide with small beak at end.

DATE	PLACE
9/00	Cape Le Grand

JULY-SEPTEMBER
COMMON

FROG HAKEA

Hakea nitida

Woodland or heath in sand or clay. Narrogin to Busselton, Albany, Eucla and Salmon Gums.
Shrub 0.5–4 m high. White to yellow flowers 10 mm long in clusters 15–25 mm across along branch. Thick, spear-shaped leaves 2–10 cm long x 5–30 mm wide with up to eight sharp teeth. Flat, oval, woody nut 25–35 mm long x 15–25 mm wide with two horns at end.

THICK-LEAVED HAKEA

Hakea pandanicarpa

DATE	PLACE
9/97	East Mount Barren
10/05	Point Ann Road

JUNE-DECEMBER
VERY COMMON

Woodland or heath. Corrigin to Cranbrook, Cape Riche, Cape Arid and Forrestania. Shrub 1–4 m high. White to green flowers (brown in bud) 15–20 mm long in clusters 2–3 cm across along branch. Thick, oblong to oval leaves 3–10 cm long x 5–30 mm wide, ending in a point. Wrinkled or knobbly, oval or egg-shaped woody nut 3–6 cm long x 2–4 cm wide with short beak at end.

CRICKET BALL HAKEA

Hakea platysperma

DATE	PLACE
9/00	Kellerberrin

AUGUST-SEPTEMBER   COMMON

Woodland or heath in sand or clay. Northampton to Corrigin, Forrestania, Boorabbin and Narembeen.
Shrub or tree 0.5–4 m high. Creamy white flowers with pink to red tinge 25 mm long in clusters 20–30 mm across. Needle-like leaves 5–15 cm long x 1–3 mm wide, ending in a long sharp point. Globular, woody nut 4–8 cm long x 4–6 cm wide.

DATE	PLACE
9/97	East Mount Barren
10/05	East Mount Barren

JUNE-OCTOBER   VERY COMMON

Heath in sand or rock. Bremer Bay to Hopetoun.
Shrub 1.5–4 m high. White to cream flowers 35–40 mm long in clusters 2–3 cm across in cup of leaves. Stiff, prickly, wavy, round to oval leaves 4–12 cm long x 4–13 cm wide, green at base of plant and yellow, orange or red near top of plant. Oval, woody nut 2–3 cm long x 15–20 mm wide, sometimes with a short beak at end.

ROYAL HAKEA

Hakea victoria

DATE	PLACE
10/98	John Forrest Track

SEPTEMBER-JANUARY
COMMON

CLUSTERED CONEFLOWER

Isopogon polycephalus

Heath in sand or gravel. Newdegate to Cape Riche, Cape Arid and Ravensthorpe.
Shrub 0.2–2 m high. White to cream flowers (woolly in bud) in globular heads 2–4 cm across, set amongst leaves along stem. Thick straight or spear-shaped leaves 10–20 cm long x 5–20 mm wide.

DATE	PLACE
10/97	Hyden

JUNE-DECEMBER   VERY COMMON

Heath in sand or gravel. Mullewa to York, Wickepin, Salmon Gums and Coolgardie.
Shrub 0.2–1 m high. White fan-shaped flowers with purple spot 4–6 mm across in spike 5–15 cm long. Straight leaves 1–6 mm long x 0.5 mm wide, curled under lengthwise and woolly at the base.

LONG-SPIKED GOODENIA
Goodenia helmsii

DATE	PLACE
9/00	John Forrest Track
10/05	Hamersley Drive

AUGUST-JANUARY AND APRIL-MAY
VERY COMMON

Heath in sand or gravel. Moora to Denmark, Cape Arid, Norseman, Narembeen and Wickepin, and Coolgardie.
Shrub 0.3–1.5 m high. White fan-shaped flowers 10–20 mm across in spike 5–10 cm long. Oblong to spear-shaped, sometimes toothed, leaves 3–7 cm long x 2–10 mm wide, mostly at base of plant.

WHITE GOODENIA
Goodenia scapigera

DATE	PLACE
9/00	Corrigin

AUGUST-NOVEMBER
COMMON

LARGE PAPER LILY

Laxmannia grandiflora

Heath in clay or gravel. Calingiri to Perth, Two Peoples Bay and Kulin, and Ravensthorpe. Herb 5–30 cm high with stilt roots 5–7 cm high. Papery white flowers 10–15 mm long in heads 10–25 mm across at end of stalk 10–20 cm long. Heads surrounded by rounded, white leaf-like lobes with brown central stripe 7–11 mm long. Grass-like leaves 10–65 mm long x 0.5–1 mm wide, all at base of plant.

DATE	PLACE
9/92	Lake Grace

AUGUST-NOVEMBER
COMMON

SHORT PAPER LILY

Laxmannia paleacea

Heath in sand. Perenjori to Wubin, and Koorda to Cranbrook, Cape Arid and Southern Cross. Herb 1–10 cm high. Papery white flowers 3–10 mm long in heads 5–15 mm across at end of stalk 2–10 cm long. Heads surrounded by rounded, brown leaf-like lobes with brown central stripe 5–8 mm long. Pointed, curved, grass-like leaves 5–15 mm long x 1 mm wide, all at base of plant.

DATE	PLACE
10/97	Lake Grace
10/05	Cape Le Grand

AUGUST–JANUARY   VERY COMMON

Heath in sand or gravel. Dongara, and Wubin to Jerramungup, Scaddan and Southern Cross.
Shrub 1.5–3 m high. White or pink flowers 10–15 mm across. Silky, oval to oblong leaves 5–10 mm long x 1–3 mm wide.

SILKY TEATREE
Leptospermum nitens

DATE	PLACE
9/92	Lake Grace

AUGUST–DECEMBER   UNCOMMON

Heath in sand or gravel. Dongara to Perth, Mount Barker, Cape Arid, Southern Cross and Kellerberrin.
Shrub 1.5-3 m high with many spiny branches 20–30 mm long. White to greenish-yellow flowers 10–15 mm across. Oval leaves 5–15 mm long x 1–4 mm wide.

SPINY TEATREE
Leptospermum spinescens

DATE	PLACE
9/00	Lucky Bay
10/05	Quaalup

JULY-DECEMBER   UNCOMMON

Heath in sand on coastal rocky hills. Cape Le Grand to Cape Arid.
Shrub 0.3–2 m high. White musky-smelling flowers (pink in bud) 5 mm long x 2–5 mm wide with woolly tips in clusters at end of branch. Veined, spear-shaped leaves 10–20 mm long and 2–5 mm wide, ending in a sharp point.

MUSKY BEARD-HEATH

Leucopogon apiculatus

DATE	PLACE
9/95	Bluff Knoll

SEPTEMBER-NOVEMBER
COMMON

DECEPTIVE STYLEWORT

Levenhookia pauciflora

Woodland in sand. Coorow, Busselton to Augusta, Lake Grace to Albany, and Wharton to Salmon Gums.
Herb 5–15 cm high. Hairy, white or pink flowers 5–10 mm long x 10 mm across on red stems 5–15 cm long. Toothed, oval leaves 3–6 mm long x 0.5–1 mm wide in a ring at top of stem, and round leaves 2–5 mm long x 2–3 mm wide at base of plant.

DATE	PLACE
12/95	Hyden

OCTOBER-FEBRUARY   VERY COMMON

Woodland in sand or clay. Kalbarri to Ongerup, Jerramungup, Forrestania and Wyalkatchem.
Shrub 1–5 m high. White to pink or purple flowers 6–8 mm long in a cylinder 10–30 mm long x 10–20 mm wide. Rough, hairy, spear-shaped leaves 5–10 mm long x 1–3 mm wide, ending in a sharp point.

CORN-EARED HONEYMYRTLE
Melaleuca adnata

DATE	PLACE
10/96	Karlgarin

AUGUST-DECEMBER
UNCOMMON

OVAL-LEAVED MICROCORYS
Microcorys obovata

Woodland and heath in sand and gravel. Moora to Koorda, and Southern Cross to Jerramungup and Munglinup.
Shrub 0.2–1.5 m high. White flowers 10–20 mm long x 10–20 mm wide. Velvety, oval leaves 5–10 mm long x 2–5 mm wide in rings of three around stem.

DATE	PLACE
10/95	John Forrest Track

MAY-JUNE AND AUGUST-FEBRUARY
UNCOMMON

Heath in sand or clay. Quairading to Albany, Cape Arid and Lake King. Shrub 25–60 cm high. White egg-shaped flowers 2–4 mm long x 2–3 mm wide in clusters 2–3 cm across at end of branches. Round, scale-like leaves 0.5–2 mm long x 0.5–2 mm wide, curled backwards against stem.

SCALY-LEAVED EVERLASTING
Ozothamnus lepidophyllum

DATE	PLACE
10/97	Lake Grace

SEPTEMBER-NOVEMBER
COMMON

SOUTHERN LAMBSWOOL
Physopsis lachnostachya

Woodland and heath in gravel. Harrismith to Kukerin, Lake King and Hyden. Shrub 0.5–1.5 m high. Woolly white flowers with yellow centres 2 mm across in a bunch 1–7 cm long x 10 mm wide. Leathery, oval or spear-shaped leaves 5–20 mm long x 1–4 mm wide, curled under lengthwise, green above and yellow below.

DATE	PLACE
9/97	Ravensthorpe
10/05	Brigadoon ?

SEPTEMBER-JANUARY   UNCOMMON

Forest, woodland and heath. Northampton to Augusta, Wharton, Southern Cross and Mullewa.
Shrub 0.1–1 m high on hairy stem. Hairy, white flowers in globular heads 15–20 mm across. Hairy, spear-shaped leaves 5–15 mm long x 1–3 mm wide.

POSY BANJINE
Pimelea imbricata

DATE	PLACE
10/96	Karlgarin
10/05	Corrigin road

JULY-DECEMBER
VERY COMMON

NATIVE FOXGLOVE
Pityrodia terminalis

Heath in sand or gravel. Billabong to Mullewa, Pingrup, Esperance, Kambalda and Cue, and Murchison.
Shrub 0.5–1 m high. White (in the south) or pink to red (in the north) tubular flowers 2 cm long in spikes 10-30 cm long at end of branches. Woolly, oval leaves 10–45 mm long x 2–10 mm wide.

DATE	PLACE
9/98	West Mount Barren

SEPTEMBER-NOVEMBER
UNCOMMON

HEATH PORANTHERA
Poranthera ericoides

Heath in sand. Carnamah, and Perth to Albany, Hopetoun and Harrismith, and Busselton.
Prostrate to erect, domed, cushion shrub 5–15 cm high. White tubular flowers 2 mm long in heads 10 mm across. Oblong leaves 2–8 mm long x 0.5–1 mm wide.

DATE	PLACE
9/97	Borden

SEPTEMBER-NOVEMBER   UNCOMMON

Forest and woodland usually after fire. Dongara to Augusta, Albany, Esperance and Borden.
Slender plant 15–50 cm high. Twenty to fifty white flowers 10 mm long x 10 mm wide in a spike 5–15 cm long on green or brown stem. Onion-like leaf 10–30 cm long x 2–4 mm wide at base of plant.

YAWNING LEEK ORCHID
Prasophyllum hians

DATE	PLACE
10/95	East Mount Barren

ROCK PAPER-HEATH

Sphenotoma squarrosum

JULY-DECEMBER
COMMON

Heath on rock or in swamps. Nannup to Augusta, Hopetoun and Borden.
Shrub 0.3–2 m high. White flowers 10 mm across in oval to globular heads 2–3 cm long and 2–3 cm across at the end of branches. Spear-shaped leaves 15–30 mm long x 1–5 mm wide, ending in a sharp point.

DATE	PLACE
9/94	Dryandra

MILKMAIDS

Stylidium caricifolium

SEPTEMBER-NOVEMBER
UNCOMMON

Woodland in gravel. Geraldton to Harvey, Kamballup and Forrestania, and Hopetoun, and Cape Arid.
Slender plant 10–35 cm high. Hairy white flowers 10–20 mm long x 10–25 mm across on hairy stem 10–30 cm long in spike 5–10 cm long. Rough, pointed, grass-like leaves 10–25 mm long x 1–5 mm wide, all at base of plant.

DATE	PLACE
10/96	Karlgarin

SEPTEMBER-DECEMBER
VERY COMMON

ROE'S FEATHERFLOWER

Verticordia roei

Heath. Beacon, Wubin, Toodyay, and Merredin to Katanning, Munglinup, Salmon Gums and Koolyanobbing.
Shrub 0.3–1.5 m high. Masses of white to cream feathery flowers (red in bud) 10–15 mm across in umbrella-shaped head on stalk 10–20 mm long at end of branches. Oblong to elliptical, three-sided leaves 1–5 mm long x 0.5–1 mm wide.

DATE	PLACE
10/96	Pallurup Rocks, Ravensthorpe

SEPTEMBER-JANUARY
VERY COMMON

FRAGRANT WAITZIA

Waitzia suaveolens

Woodland. Jurien to Augusta, Cape Arid, Balladonia and Kellerberrin.
Slender plant 30–60 cm high. White flowers (pink in bud) with yellow centres 10–20 mm long x 10–30 mm across, surrounded by papery, pointed (not toothed) white leaf-like lobes, in loose group at end of branch. Oblong leaves 1–10 cm long x 1–10 mm wide.

STIFF WESTRINGIA
Westringia rigida

DATE	PLACE
10/96	Karlgarin
10/05	Hopetoun

APRIL-JANUARY
VERY COMMON

Woodland and heath in sand. Goomalling to Ongerup, Eucla and Laverton. Shrub 0.1–1.5 m high. Hairy white or pink flowers 10–15 mm long x 10–15 mm wide. Rough, hairy (when new), pointed, oblong leaves 3–10 mm long x 1 mm wide, curled under lengthwise.

DWARF GRASSTREE
Xanthorrhoea nana

DATE	PLACE
10/97	Harrismith

JULY-OCTOBER
VERY COMMON

Woodland and heath in sand. Jurien to Collie, Newdegate, Boorabbin and Beacon. Shrub 0.5–1 m high. White flowers 5–10 mm long in a green spike 25–30 cm long x 3–7 cm wide, bent to the side. Grass-like, four-sided leaves 0.5–1 m long x 1–3 mm wide at top of trunk.

DATE	PLACE
8/98	Paynes Find

AUGUST-OCTOBER   UNCOMMON

Woodland and heath, especially near salt lakes and granite outcrops. Mullewa to Cranbrook, Bremer Bay, Ravensthorpe and Paynes Find.
Slender plant 5–30 cm high. One or two green flowers 3–5 cm long and 1–3 cm wide with purple stripes, red lumps on lip and thickened yellow tips to two petals. Hairy, grass-like leaf 5–15 cm long x 10 mm wide at base of plant.

PURPLE-VEINED SPIDER ORCHID
Caladenia doutchiae

DATE	PLACE
8/96	Hyden

AUGUST-OCTOBER   COMMON

Woodland, heath and granite outcrops. Kalbarri to Kojonup, Salmon Gums, Coolgardie and Paynes Find.
Slender plant 10–30 cm high. One to three green flowers 3–4 cm long and 2–3 cm wide with red stripes, and black lumps on lip. Hairy, grass-like leaf 5–15 cm long x 5 mm wide at base of plant.

JACK IN THE BOX ORCHID
Caladenia roei

BALD ISLAND MARLOCK
Eucalyptus conferruminata

DATE	PLACE
9/00	*Frenchman Peak*

JULY-NOVEMBER
UNCOMMON

Woodland in sand on rocky hills. Albany to Cape Arid and Ravensthorpe.
Tree 2–8 m high. Green to yellowish green flowers 3–6 cm long x 11 cm wide with finger-like buds 3–5 cm long on a broad strap 2–4 cm long. Spear-shaped leaves 4–8 cm long x 1–2 cm wide.

BLACK TOOTHBRUSHES
Grevillea hookeriana

DATE	PLACE
12/95	*Corrigin*

AUGUST-FEBRUARY
UNCOMMON

Woodland and heath. Morawa to Brookton, Gnowangerup, Kalgoorlie, Menzies and Merredin.
Shrub 1.5–3 m high. Silky green and black to purple (rarely red, pink or yellow) flowers 15–25 mm long in spike 2–8 cm long on one side of branch. Straight, pointed, simple or divided leaves 5–15 cm long x 1–2 mm wide.

DATE	PLACE
9/00	Moir Track

JULY-SEPTEMBER
VERY COMMON

CAULIFLOWER HAKEA
Hakea corymbosa

Woodland and heath in sand. Darkan to Denmark, Cape Arid and Hyden.
Shrub 0.5–2 m high. Green to yellowish green flowers 15–35 mm long in clusters 10–30 mm across, often forming dense umbrella-shaped head. Prickly, oblong leaves 2–12 cm long x 2–10 mm wide, ending in a sharp point. Egg-shaped, woody nut 2–3 cm long x 15–20 mm wide with short thick beak at end.

DATE	PLACE
9/97	East Mount
	Barren

AUGUST-NOVEMBER
COMMON

BLACK CORAL PEA
Kennedia nigricans

Woodland and heath. Cape Riche to Hopetoun, and Cape Arid.
Climbing vine with stems 4–5 m long. Black and yellow pea flowers 3–4 cm long x 5–10 mm wide. Oval leaves 2–10 cm long x 2–8 cm wide.

SPOON-LEAVED MULLA MULLA
Ptilotus spathulatus

DATE	PLACE
10/95	Dryandra

AUGUST-NOVEMBER
COMMON

Woodland. Northampton to Wellstead, Caiguna and Koolyanobbing.
Prostrate shrub 1–25 cm high. Green to white or yellow hairy flowers in a cone or cylinder 1–10 cm long x 1–3 cm across, turned up at the end of stems 5–20 cm long forming circle on the ground at base of plant. Spoon-shaped leaves 5–15 mm long x 2–4 mm wide along stem, and 4–6 cm long x 6–8 mm wide at base of plant.

WINGED STACKHOUSIA
Tripterococcus brunonis

DATE	PLACE
10/97	Lake Grace
10/05	Hyden
8/06	Brigadoon

JUNE-FEBRUARY   UNCOMMON

Forest and heath in sand. Kalbarri to Augusta, Cape Arid and Coolgardie.
Slender plant 10–80 cm high. Blackish or greenish yellow flowers 10–15 mm across in a spike 5–10 cm long at end of stem. Few, oblong leaves 2–20 mm long x 0.5 mm wide.

DATE	PLACE
9/00	Ravensthorpe
10/05	Pabelup Drive
09/07	Miling

AUGUST-JANUARY
COMMON

LILAC HIBISCUS
Alyogyne huegelii

Woodland. Shark Bay to Augusta and Beacon, and Kulin to Albany, Cape Arid and Forrestania.
Shrub 1–3 m high. Lilac to purple flowers 3–15 cm across. Crinkled, hairy, oval leaves 0.5–10 cm long x 1–10 cm wide, divided into three to five 3-toothed fingers 5–50 mm long x 1–20 mm wide.

DATE	PLACE
10/92	Salt River Road
10/05	Cape Le Grand

AUGUST-OCTOBER
COMMON

NARROW-LEAVED SQUILL
Chamaescilla spiralis

Woodland and heath in damp sand. Coorow to Mundaring, Albany, Esperance and Quairading, and Augusta.
Herb 15–35 cm high. Blue flowers 15–20 mm across in a head on a red stalk 10–30 cm long. Nine to twenty flat, oblong leaves 6–8 cm long x 2–4 mm wide, all at base of plant.

DATE	PLACE
10/95	John Forrest Track

AUGUST-DECEMBER   UNCOMMON

Woodland and heath. Kalbarri to Merredin, Albany, Cape Arid, Zanthus and Yalgoo.
Climbing vine 0.2–2.5 m high. Up to ten purple or blue flowers 15–30 mm across on a stalk 1–4 cm long. Oblong or spear-shaped leaves 2–40 mm long x 0.5–1 mm wide.

MANY-HEADED BLUE CREEPER
Cheiranthera filifolia

DATE	PLACE
8/96	Hyden

JULY-NOVEMBER   UNCOMMON

Woodland and heath in sand or gravel. Brookton to Wagin, Kamballup, Lake King and Southern Cross.
Shrub 30–90 cm high. Many silky blue to white flowers 3–5 mm long x 3 mm wide in spikes 30–50 cm long x 1 cm wide. Needle-like leaves 5–10 mm long x 0.5 mm wide, ending in a sharp point.

NEEDLE-LEAVED BLUE SMOKEBUSH
Conospermum croniniae

DATE	PLACE
8/96	Hyden

AUGUST-OCTOBER
UNCOMMON

WESTERN TINY BLUE ORCHID
Cyanicula caerulea subsp. *apertala*

Woodland and heath. Hyden to Ongerup, Bremer Bay and Cape Arid. Slender plant 5–15 cm high. One blue flower 2 cm across. Hairy, spear-shaped leaf 3–5 cm long x 5 mm wide at base of plant.

DATE	PLACE
10/97	Lake Grace

AUGUST-DECEMBER   UNCOMMON

Woodland and heath in sand and gravel. Perenjori to Jurien, and Northam to Dumbleyung, Lake King and Merredin. Shrub 0.5–2 m high. Sticky, hairy, purple or blue flowers with papery wings 10–15 mm across. Usually sticky, toothed, spear shaped leaves 15–50 mm long x 2–10 mm wide.

LANCE-LEAVED TINSEL FLOWER
Cyanostegia lanceolata

DATE	PLACE
9/92	Tarin Rock, Lake Grace
10/05	Ongerup road

JULY-NOVEMBER   VERY COMMON

Heath. Eneabba to Albany, Hopetoun, Koolyanobbing and Perenjori, and Rocky Gully and Coolgardie.
Shrub 10–60 cm high with many thin, reed-like stems. Blue to purple flowers (woolly grey-black in bud) 10–20 mm across. No leaves or oblong to spear-shaped leaves 5–50 mm long x 1–20 mm wide.

RUSH-LIKE DAMPIERA
Dampiera juncea

DATE	PLACE
10/98	Ravensthorpe
10/05	Nuts of Orleans Bay

JULY-DECEMBER
COMMON

POUCHED DAMPIERA
Dampiera sacculata

Heath in sand or gravel. Koorda to Darkan, Albany, Cape Arid and Lake King, and Busselton to Augusta.
Shrub 10–40 cm high with many thin, four-sided, reed-like stems. Blue to purple flowers (woolly grey in bud, with lump at bottom) 10 mm across, on stalk 1–3 cm long. Oblong leaves 10–45 mm long x 1–2 mm wide.

DATE	PLACE
10/97	Dryandra

SEPTEMBER-DECEMBER   VERY COMMON

Woodland in sand or gravel. Mullewa to Brookton, Cranbrook, Salmon Gums, Kalgoorlie and Yalgoo.
Shrub 10–40 cm high. Blue to purple flowers (woolly white in bud) 10 mm across at end of woolly stalks 5–25 cm long. Spoon-shaped leaves 5–15 cm long x 10–30 mm wide, glossy green above and woolly grey-white below, all at base of plant.

WOOLLY-HEADED DAMPIERA
Dampiera eriocephala

DATE	PLACE
9/92	Tarin Rock,
	Lake Grace

SEPTEMBER-DECEMBER
VERY COMMON

WELLS' DAMPIERA
Dampiera wellsiana

Heath. Mullewa to Katanning, Salmon Gums and Murchison.
Shrub 5–25 cm high. Many blue flowers 5 mm across, in dense woolly heads 2–6 cm long x 10–20 mm across at the end of woolly stalks 5–20 cm long. Fleshy, spoon-shaped leaves 3–10 cm long x 5–40 mm wide, all at base of plant.

WINGED-LEAF DAMPIERA
Dampiera decurrens

DATE	PLACE
9/00	Lucky Bay

SEPTEMBER-OCTOBER
RARE

Heath in sand on granite rocks. Cape Le Grand.
Shrub 0.1–1 m high. Blue flowers (woolly grey in bud) 10–15 mm across. Toothed, spear-shaped leaves 1–5 cm long x 2–25 mm wide, continuing down stem as wings.

CLAW LESCHENAULTIA
Lechenaultia heteromera

DATE	PLACE
9/00	East Mount Barren

AUGUST-DECEMBER
COMMON

Heath in sand. Lake King to Bremer Bay, Munglinup and Salmon Gums.
Erect spindly shrub 25–80 cm high. Blue and white flowers 10–20 mm across in irregular clusters. Hooked, needle-like leaves 3–10 mm long x 0.5–1 mm wide, ending in a sharp point.

DATE	PLACE
12/90	Fitzgerald River National Park

AUGUST-APRIL
UNCOMMON

COMMON BLUE GOODENIA
Goodenia caerulea

Heath in sand or gravel. Kalbarri to Augusta, Hopetoun, Narembeen and Mullewa. Shrub 10–50 cm high with many rough, sometimes hairy, stems. Single blue and white or yellow flowers 15 mm across on stalks 10–25 mm long widely spaced on stem. Broad leaves 10–15 mm long x 1 mm wide along stem, and 3–7 cm long x 1–3 mm wide, sometimes with a few teeth, at base of plant.

DATE	PLACE
12/90	Fitzgerald River National Park

SEPTEMBER-JANUARY   UNCOMMON

Woodland and heath in sand or clay. Beacon to Wubin, and Mundaring to Dunsborough, Albany, Cape Arid and Boorabbin.
Shrub 5–30 cm high with rough white stem. Blue flowers (woolly grey-green in bud) 10–20 mm across in spike 5–20 cm long. Rough, velvety, broad to spear-shaped leaves 10–15 cm long x 1–4 mm wide along stem, and 3–7 cm long x 5–10 mm wide at base of plant.

HOARY GOODENIA
Goodenia incana

DENSE-LEAVED EREMOPHILA
Eremophila densifolia

DATE	PLACE
9/00	Ravensthorpe

SEPTEMBER-NOVEMBER
COMMON

Woodland. Southern Cross to Newdegate, Jerramungup, Munglinup and 100 mile Tank. Shrub 15–75 cm high. Purple to blue or pink tubular flowers 10–15 mm long x 10 mm wide in bunch near end of branch. Rough, dark brown-green, oblong to needle-like leaves 5–20 mm long x 1–2 mm wide, ending in a point.

STICKY HALGANIA
Halgania andromedifolia

DATE	PLACE
9/00	Ravensthorpe

AUGUST-MARCH   VERY COMMON

Woodland in sand or clay. Mukinbudin to Forrestania, Lake Grace, Cape Riche, Eucla, Balladonia and Kalgoorlie.
Shrub 0.1–2 m high. Blue star flowers 10–15 mm across with yellow or purple centres. Sometimes sticky, sometimes silky, oblong to spear shaped leaves 5–25 mm long x 2–4 mm wide, curled under lengthwise, glossy green above and woolly white below.

109

DATE	PLACE
12/90	Fitzgerald River National Park
10/05	Point Ann

SEPTEMBER-JUNE   UNCOMMON

Woodland and heath in sand. Eneabba to Augusta, Cape Arid, Forrestania, Rocky Gully and Narrogin.
Shrub 0.1–1 m high. Purple or blue pea flowers 10–15 mm across in clusters 2–5 cm across at ends of branches. Crowded, blunt, needle-like leaves 10–15 mm long x 0.25 mm wide.

PURPLE PEA
Gompholobium confertum

DATE	PLACE
9/97	Red Gum Pass

SEPTEMBER-DECEMBER
UNCOMMON

HANDSOME WEDGE-PEA
Gompholobium venustum

Woodland and heath in sand or gravel. Walpole to Hopetoun and Cranbrook. Upright or sprawling shrub 10–50 cm high. Blue or purple and pink pea flowers 10–15 mm across in clusters 3–5 cm across at end of stalk 5 cm long. Nine to twenty one, pointed, oblong leaflets 5–20 mm long x 1 mm wide in pairs along leaf.

DATE	PLACE
10/97	Lake Grace

SEPTEMBER-OCTOBER   UNCOMMON

Heath in sand. Brookton to Pingrup, Hyden and Southern Cross.
Shrub 20–80 cm high. Blue, purple or pink flowers (velvety grey in bud) 10 mm long x 10 mm wide. Silky or leathery, oblong to spoon-shaped leaves 5–10 mm long x 1–2 mm wide with star-shaped hairs on velvety young leaves.

STAR-HAIRED MICROCORYS
Microcorys sp. *stellate*

DATE	PLACE
8/96	Corrigin
10/05	Wandoo

PURPLE MIRBELIA
Mirbelia floribunda

JULY-OCTOBER
UNCOMMON

Woodland in sand or gravel. Mullewa to Geraldton, Armadale, Borden, Lake King and Westonia, and Esperance.
Upright or sprawling shrub 10–60 cm high. Purple or blue pea flowers (hairy white in bud) 10–15 mm across. Needle-like leaves 3–10 mm long x 1 mm wide, opposite or in threes, curled under lengthwise and with sharp hook at end.

111

DATE	PLACE
10/89	Stirling Range National Park

SEPTEMBER-DECEMBER
UNCOMMON

FRINGED DAISY BUSH

Olearia ciliata

Forest and woodland in sand or gravel. Jurien, and Dunsborough, and Kukerin to Denmark, Cape Arid and Lake King, and Boorabbin.
Shrub 15–40 cm high. Round purple to blue or white flowers 20–25 mm across with yellow centres on stalk 10–30 cm long. Hairy, pointed, spear-shaped leaves 5–15 mm long x 1–2 mm wide, with curled edges.

DATE	PLACE
9/97	Wellstead

SEPTEMBER-NOVEMBER
UNCOMMON

AZURE SUN ORCHID

Thelymitra azurea

Woodland in sand or clay. Wongan Hills to Cranbrook, Bremer Bay, Eucla and Lake King. Slender plant 10–40 cm high. Two to fifteen blue flowers 2–3 cm across grouped at top of stem. Grass-like leaf 10–25 cm long x 5 mm wide at base of plant.

DATE	PLACE
12/90	Fitzgerald River National Park

OCTOBER-MAY   UNCOMMON

Forest and woodland. Shark Bay to Augusta, Cape Arid and Wyalkatchem, and Boorabbin and Koolyanobbing. Shrub 0.1–1 m high with many thick stems, either smooth or hairy near base. Purple feathery-edged flowers 15–30 mm across, with seven pins in centre, three straight 2–6 mm long and four curved 7–10 mm long. No leaves.

BROOM FRINGE LILY
Thysanotus sparteus

DATE	PLACE
10/97	Lake Grace

SEPTEMBER-DECEMBER
UNCOMMON

POSY FRINGE LILY
Thysanotus triandrus

Forest, woodland and heath in sand or gravel. Eneabba to Augusta, Cape Arid, Hyden and York. Shrub 5–45 cm high. Five to fifty purple feathery-edged flowers 15–25 mm across, with four curved pins in centre, three 5 mm long and one 10 mm long, in an umbrella-shaped head 3–5 cm across at end of stalk 10–40 cm long. Many woolly or hairy, grass-like leaves 5–45 cm long x 1–3 mm wide, all at base of plant.

List of multi-coloured wildflowers

Red flowers

Coastal Jug Flower	21
Cayley's Banksia	21
Hairy Triggerplant	32
Crab Claws	33
Orange Flame Pea	38
Orange Rattle Pea	39
Reverse-leaf Daviesia	39
Prickly Parrot Pea	40
Wheel Sundew	40
Box Poison	42
Berry Poison	42
Prickly Poison	43
Yorkrakine Grevillea	45
Leathery-leaved Pea	45
Pins and Needles	46
Mop Bushpea	46
Flat Flag Rush	47
Ouch Bush	57
Needle Tree	62
Nerved Bush Pea	71
Prostrate Globe Pea	72
Boomerang Triggerplant	72
Large Waxflower	78
Cricket Ball Hakea	84
Purple-veined Spider Orchid	97
Jack in the Box Orchid	97
Black Toothbrushes	98

Pink flowers

Little Woollybush	2
Wheatbelt Woollybush	2
Veined-leaf Jug Flower	3
Spoon-leaved Cranberry	5
Lazy Spider Orchid	9
Needle-leaved Flame Pea	10
Warty Bush	11
Splendid Foxglove	11
Huegel's Grevillea	12
Wax Grevillea	14
Woolly Red Grevillea	14
Zig-zag Flowered Grevillea	15
Comb-leaved Grevillea	16
Three-lobed Grevillea	16
Four-winged Mallee	18
Orange Flame Pea	38
Wheel Sundew	40
Berry Poison	42
Pins and Needles	46
Needle Tree	62
Oval-leaved Myrtle	76
Large Waxflower	78
Crab Smokebush	79
Australian Bindweed	80
Pallurup Grevillea	81
Gilbert's Hakea	83
Cricket Ball Hakea	84
Silky Teatree	88
Musky Beard-heath	89
Deceptive Stylewort	89
Corn-eared Honeymyrtle	90
Native Foxglove	92
Fragrant Waitzia	95
Stiff Westringia	96
Black Toothbrushes	98
Dense-leaved Eremophila	108
Sticky Halgania	108
Handsome Wedge-pea	109
Star-haired Microcorys	110

Orange flowers
Granite Woollybush	3
Hairy Sheoak	5
Needle-leaved Flame Pea	10
Huegel's Grevillea	12
Red Toothbrushes	13
Red Leschenaultia	18
Bitter Quandong	20
Ouch Bush	57
Rusty Dryandra	60
Oak-leaved Dryandra	61
Prostrate Globe Pea	72

Brown flowers
Esperance King Spider Orchid	8
Tennis Ball Banksia	53
Southern Plains Banksia	54
Teasel Banksia	54
Ouch Bush	57
Elegant Donkey Orchid	58
Bee Orchid	58
Rusty Dryandra	60
Shining Honeypot	60
Oak-leaved Dryandra	61
Thick-leaved Hakea	84

Yellow flowers
Fringed Mantis Orchid	8
Needle-leaved Flame Pea	10
Huegel's Grevillea	12
Zig-zag Flowered Grevillea	15
Three-lobed Grevillea	16
Red Leschenaultia	18
Qualup Bell	19
Bitter Quandong	20
Gardner's Coneflower	27
Nodding Coneflower	27
Needle-leaved Triggerplant	32
Woolly Banksia	37
Violet Banksia	37
Reverse-leaf Bitter Pea	39
Prickly Parrot Pea	40
Golden Dryandra	41
Box Poison	42
Berry Poison	42
Prickly Poison	43
Curly Grevillea	44
Orange Flame Grevillea	44
Yorkrakine Grevillea	45
Leathery-leaved Pea	45
Pins and Needles	46
Mop Bushpea	46
Frog Hakea	83
Spiny Teatree	88
Southern Lambswool	91
Purple-veined Spider Orchid	97
Bald Island Marlock	98
Black Toothbrushes	98
Cauliflower Hakea	99
Black Coral Pea	99
Spoon-leaved Mulla Mulla	100

White flowers

Veined-leaf Jug Flower	3
Wax Grevillea	14
Bitter Quandong	20
Cayley's Banksia	21
Mountain Boronia	23
Fringed Waxflower	24
Pearly Sundew	25
Coastal Hakea	26
Nodding Coneflower	27
Hairy Teatree	29
Silver Teatree	29
Coast Velvet Bush	31
Splendid Featherflower	34
Dainty Featherflower	34
Striking Pink Featherflower	35
Painted Featherflower	36
Woolly Banksia	37
Wheel Sundew	40
Fan Hakea	43
Leathery-leaved Pea	45
Pins and Needles	46
Spreading Fringe Leaf	47
Spider Smokebush	55
Starburst Cottonheads	56
Long-leaved Petrophile	67
Slender Phebalium	71
Boomerang Triggerplant	72
Yellow Mountain Triggerplant	73
Maize Triggerplant	73
Spoon-leaved Mulla Mulla	100
Needle-leaved Blue Smokebush	102
Claw Leschenaultia	106
Fringed Daisy Bush	111

Green/Black flowers

Fringed Mantis Orchid	8
Qualup Bell	19
Bitter Quandong	20
Violet Banksia	37
Baxter's Banksia	52
Showy Banksia	52
Lemann's Banksia	53
Tennis Ball Banksia	53
Sunny Rainbow	59
Oak-leaved Dryandra	61
Needle Tree	62
Barrel Coneflower	65
Thick-leaved Hakea	84
Spiny Teatree	88

Blue/Purple flowers

Red Kangaroo Paw	1
Little Bottlebrush	22
Pink Starflower	23
Common Coopernookia	24
Brilliant Kunzea	28
Slender Kunzea	28
Rough Honeymyrtle	30
Small Regelia	31
Leafless Tetratheca	36
Violet Banksia	37
Curly Grevillea	44
Nerved Bush Pea	71
Maize Triggerplant	73
Bell Creeper	77
Large Waxflower	78
Blue-eyed Smokebush	78
Crab Smokebush	79
Corn-eared Honeymyrtle	90
Purple-veined Spider Orchid	97
Black Toothbrushes	98

Index

Acacia acuminata	48	*Beaufortia micrantha*	22
bifaria	49	orbifolia	10
cedroides	75	schaueri	22
erinacea	50	Bell Qualup	19
glaucoptera	49	*Billardiera coriacea*	77
lasiocalyx	48	Bindweed Australian	80
multispicata	50	Boronia Mountain	23
nigricans	51	*Boronia albiflora*	23
trigonophylla	51	Bottlebrush Granite	19
Adenanthos argyreus	2	Little	22
cuneatus	21	Pink	22
flavidiflorus	2	Ravensthorpe	10
sericeus subsp. *sphalma*	3		
venosus	3	*Caladenia decora*	8
Agonis spathulata	75	doutchiae	97
Allocasuarina campestris	4	falcata	8
microstachya	4	multiclavia	9
pinaster	38	pulchra	9
trichodon	5	roei	97
Alyogyne huegelii	101	saccharata	77
Anarthria scabra	47	*Calothamnus macrocarpus*	6
Anigozanthus rufus	1	pinifolius	6
Anthocercis fasciculata	76	validus	7
Anthotium Red	1	villosus	7
Anthotium rubra	1	*Calytrix decandra*	23
Astroloma compactum	5	*Chamaescilla spiralis*	101
		Chamaexeros fimbriata	47
Baeckea ovalifolia	76	*Chamelaucium ciliatum*	24
Banjine Posy	92	megalopetalum	78
Banksia Baxter's	52	*Cheiranthera filifolia*	102
Cayley's	21	*Chloanthes coccinea*	11
Lemann's	53	*Chorizema aciculare*	10
Showy	52	glycinifolium	38
Southern Plains	54	Clawflower Barrens	7
Teasel	54	Dense	6
Tennis Ball	53	Large-fruited	6
Violet	37	Woolly	7
Woolly	37	Compass Bush	38
Banksia baxteri	52	Cone Bush Golden	55
baueri	37	Coneflower Barrel	65
caleyi	21	Clustered	85
laevigata	53	Gardner's	27
lemanniana	53	Nodding	27
media	54	Woolly	65
pulchella	54	*Conospermum brownii*	78
speciosa	52	croniniae	102
violacea	37	distichum	79
Beard-heath Musky	89	ephedroides	79
		teretifolium	55

Conostylis petrophiloides	56
phathyrantha	56
vaginata	57
Conothamnus aureaus	55
Convolvulus erubsecens	80
Coopernookia Common	24
Coopernookia polygalacea	24
Cottonheads Sandplain	56
Sheath	57
Starburst	56
Crab Claws	33
Cranberry Spoon-leaved	5
Creeper Bell	77
Cryptandra Spiny	80
Cryptandra pungens	80
Cyanicula caerulea subsp. *apertala*	103
Cyanostegia lanceolata	103
Daisy Bush Fringed	111
Dampiera Pouched	104
Rush-like	104
Wells'	105
Winged-leaf	106
Woolly-headed	105
Dampiera decurrens	106
eriocephala	105
juncea	104
sacculata	104
wellsiana	105
Daviesia alternifolia	39
incrassata subsp. *reversifolia*	39
pachyphylla	57
Dillwinyia pungens	40
Diuris concinna	58
laxiflora	58
Drosera leucoblasta	40
pycnoblasta	25
subhirtella	59
Dryandra Golden	41
Oak-leaved	61
Rusty	60
Dryandra ferruginea	60
nobilis	41
obtusa	60
quercifolia	61
Eremaea Common	41
Eremaea pauciflora	41
Eremophila Dense-leaved	108
Eremophila densifolia	108

Eucalyptus conferruminata	98
pleurocarpa	81
preissiana	59
tetraptera	18
Everlasting Scaly-leaved	91
Featherflower Dainty	34
Golden	74
Hook-leaf	35
Painted	36
Roe's	95
Splendid	34
Striking Pink	35
Flame Pea Needle-leaved	10
Orange	38
Foxglove Native	92
Splendid	11
Fringe Leaf Spreading	47
Fringe Lily Broom	112
Posy	112
Gastrolobium parviflorum	42
parvifolium	42
spinosum	43
Glischrocaryon aureum	61
Gompholobium confertum	109
marginatum	62
scabrum	25
venustum	109
Goodenia Common Blue	107
Hoary	107
Long-spiked	86
Silver	63
Smooth	63
White	86
Goodenia affinis	63
caerulea	107
helmsii	86
incana	107
leavis	63
scapigera	86
Grasstree Dwarf	96
Grevillea Comb-leaved	16
Curly	44
Huegel's	12
Orange Flame	44
Pallurup	81
Star-leaf	12
Three-lobed	16
Trailing	15
Wax	14
Woolly Red	14
Yorkrakine	45
Zig-zag Flowered	15

Grevillea asteriscosa	12
cagiana	13
eryngioides	44
excelsior	44
hookeriana	98
huegelii	12
insignis	14
nudiflora	15
patentiloba	15
pectinata	16
pilosa	14
prostrata	81
tetragonoloba	13
tripartita	16
yorkrakinensis	45
Guinea Flower Cushion	64
Hakea Cauliflower	99
Coastal	26
Cricket Ball	84
Fan	43
Frog	83
Gilbert's	83
Grass-leaf	26
Royal	85
Rusty	82
Swan-fruit	82
Thick-leaved	84
Hakea brownii	43
clavata	26
corymbosa	99
cygna	82
ferruginea	82
gilbertii	83
multilineata	26
nitida	83
pandanicarpa	84
platysperma	84
preissii	62
victoria	85
Halgania Sticky	108
Halgania andromedifolia	108
Hibbertia Prickly	64
Hibbertia enervia	64
mucronata	64
Hibiscus Lilac	101
Honeymyrtle Corky	30
Corn-eared	90
Lemon	66
Needle-leaved	66
Rough	30
Honeypot Shining	60
Honeysuckle Holly-leaved	67

Isopogon gardneri	27
polycephalus	85
teretifolius	27
trilobus	65
villosus	65
Jug Flower Veined-leaf	3
Coastal	21
Kangaroo Paw Red	1
Kennedia nigricans	99
Kunzea Baxter's	17
Granite	17
Showy	28
Slender	28
Kunzea affinis	28
baxteri	17
jucunda	28
pulchella	17
Lambertia ilicifolia	67
Lambswool Southern	91
Lasiopetalum discolor	31
Laxmannia grandiflora	87
paleacea	87
Lechenaultia formosa	18
heteromera	106
Leptospermum nitens	88
roei	29
sericeum	29
spinescens	88
Leschenaultia Claw	106
Red	18
Leucopogon apiculatus	89
Levenhookia pauciflora	89
Mallee Bell-fruited	59
Four-winged	18
Many-headed Blue Creeper	102
Marlock Bald Island	98
Melaleuca adnata	90
citrina	66
elliptica	19
pungens	66
scabra	30
suberosa	30
Microcorys Oval-leaved	90
Star-haired	110
Microcorys obovata	90
sp. *stellate*	110
Milkmaids	94
Mirbelia Purple	110
Mirbelia floribunda	110

Mulla Mulla Spoon-leaved	100	Pins and Needles	46
Myrtle Oval-leaved	76	*Pityrodia exserta*	11
Needle Tree	62	*pityrodia*	92
Nemcia coriacea	45	Poison Berry	42
		Box	42
Olearia ciliata	111	Prickly	43
Orchid Azure Sun	111	Popflower Common	61
Bee	58	Poranthera Heath	93
Elegant Donkey	58	*Poranthera ericoides*	93
Esperance King Spider	8	*Prasophyllum hians*	93
Fringed Mantis	8	*Ptilotus spathulatus*	100
Jack in the Box	97	*Pultenaea neurocalyx*	71
Lazy Spider	9		
Purple-veined Spider	97	Quandong Bitter	20
Slender Spider	9		
Western Tiny Blue	103	Rainbow Sunny	59
Yawning Leek	93	Raspberry Jam	48
Ouch Bush	57	Regelia Barrens	20
Ozothamnus lepidophyllum	91	Small	31
		Regelia inops	31
Paintbrushes Red	13	*velutina*	20
Painted Lady	25	Rush Flat Flag	47
Paper-heath Rock	94		
Paper Lily Large	87	*Santalum murrayanum*	20
Short	87	Sheoak Bloated	4
Pea Black and Gold	62	Hairy	5
Black Coral	99	Smokebush Blue-eyed	78
Handsome Wedge	109	Crab	79
Leathery-leaved	45	Fine-leaf	79
Mop Bush	46	Needle-leaved Blue	102
Nerved Bush	71	Spider	55
Orange Rattle	39	Snottygobble Grooved-leaf	70
Prickly Parrot	40	Needle-leaved	70
Prostrate Globe	72	*Sphaerolobium linophyllum*	72
Purple	109	*Sphenotoma squarrosum*	94
Reverse-leaf Bitter	39	Squill Narrow-leaved	101
Peppermint Spoon-leaved	75	Stackhousia Winged	100
Persoonia saundersiana	70	Starflower Pink	23
teretifolia	70	Stylewort Deceptive	89
Petrophile Blue-leaved	69	*Stylidium breviscapum*	72
Fine-leaved	68	*caricifolium*	94
Long-leaved	67	*dichotomum*	46
Needle-leaved	68	*galioides*	73
Pineapple	69	*hirsutum*	32
Petrophile brevifolia	68	*leptophyllum*	32
ericifolia	68	*macranthum*	33
fastigiata	69	*pilosum*	33
glauca	69	*squamellosum*	73
longifolia	67	Sundew Pearly	25
Phebalium Slender	71	Wheel	40
Phebalium filifolium	71		
Physopsis lachnostachya	91	Tailflower Mountain	76
Pimelea imbricata	92	Tallarack	81
physodes	19	Tamma	4

Teatree Hairy	29
Silky	88
Silver	29
Spiny	88
Tetratheca Leafless	36
Tetratheca efoliata	36
Thelymitra azurea	111
Thysanotus sparteus	112
triandrus	112
Tinsel Flower Lance-leaved	103
Toothbrushes Black	98
Red	13
Triggerplant Boomerang	72
Hairy	32
Maize	73
Needle-leaved	32
Silky	33
Yellow Mountain	73
Tripterococcus brunonis	100
Urodon dasyphyllus	46
Velvet Bush Coast	31
Verticordia brachypoda	34
chrysanthella	74
inclusa	34
insignis	35
pennigera	35
picta	36
roei	95
Villarsia	74
Villarsia parnassifolia	74
Waitzia Fragrant	95
Waitzia suaveolens	95
Warty Bush	11
Wattle Barrens	75
Dome	50
Esperance	51
Flat	49
Hedgehog	50
Silver	48
Small Flat	49
Triangle-leaved	51
Waxflower Fringed	24
Large	78
Westringia Stiff	96
Westringia rigida	96
Woollybush Granite	3
Little	2
Wheatbelt	2
Xanthorrhoea nana	96

Selected Reading

Bennett, E.M. *Common and Aboriginal Names of Western Australian Plant Species.* 2nd Edition. Glen Forrest: Wildflower Society of Western Australia (1991).

Blackall, W.E., and Grieve, B.J. *How to Know Western Australian Wildflowers.* Parts 1-4. Nedlands: University of Western Australia Press (1954-1982).

Corrick, M.G., Fuhrer, B.A., and George, A.S. *Wildflowers of Southern Western Australia.* Noble Park, Victoria: Five Mile Press (1996).

Erickson, R., George, A.S., Marchant, N.G., and Morcombe, M.K. *Flowers and Plants of Western Australia.* Sydney: Reed (1973).

Grieve, B.J. *How to Know Western Australian Wildflowers.* Part 2. 2nd Edition. Nedlands: University of Western Australia Press (1998).

Hoffman, N., and Brown, A. *Orchids of South-West Australia.* Revised 2nd Edition. Nedlands: University of Western Australia Press (1998).

Marchant, N.G., Wheeler, J.R., Rye, B.L., Bennett, E.M., Lander, N.S., and Macfarlane, T.D. *Flora of the Perth Region.* Perth: Western Australian Herbarium (1987).

Nevill, S., and McQuoid, N. *Guide to the Wildflowers of South Western Australia.* Perth: Simon Nevill Publications (1998).